The Healthy Bird Cookbook

A Lifesaving
Nutritional Guide
& Recipe Collection

**Robin
Deutsch**

T.F.H. Publications, Inc.
One TFH Plaza
Third and Union Avenues
Neptune City, NJ 07753

This book has been published with the intent to provide accurate and authoritative information in regard to the subject matter within. While every precaution has been taken in preparation of this book, the publisher and author assume no responsibility for errors or omissions. Neither is any liability assumed for damages resulting from the use of the information herein.

Library of Congress Cataloging-in-Publication Data
Deutsch, Robin.
The healthy bird cookbook : a lifesaving nutritional guide and recipe collection / Robin Deutsch.
p. cm.
Includes index.
ISBN 0-7938-0538-4 (alk. paper)
1. Cage birds-Feeding and feeds-Recipes. 2. Cage birds-Nutrition. I. Title.
SF461.75.D48 2004
636.6'8–dc22
2003027383

All photos by Robin Deutsch and T.F.H. photo archives
Cover design by Candida Moreira Tómassini
Book design by Mary Ann Mahon Kahn.

www.tfh.com

Contents

Part Two:
The Recipes

Chapter 6
Breads and Muffins

Chapter 8
Eggs and Omelets

Chapter 9
Pastas and Pizzas

Chapter 10
Rice and Noodle Dishes

Chapter 14
Mash Diets 161

Chapter 15
Fruit Dishes, Desserts, and Treats 165

DEDICATION:
To my wonderful husband, Steve, for putting up
with all of my birds. To my children , Marcy and Scott,
for all of their help. To my parents, Harriet and Bernard Cohen,
for starting me on my love for birds when they bought
me my first bird when I was seven. Little did anyone
know where it would lead.

Foreword

Twenty-five years ago, my husband and I bought our very first bird together, Charlie, an Amazon parrot. Charlie was very wild back then and hated people, and he was also very sick. He was loaded with all kinds of parasites and even E. coli. We almost lost him, and we would have, if it wasn't for our veterinarian.

Fortunately, our veterinarian at that time was Dr. Theodore Lafeber, one of the early pioneers in the avian field. While most people thought that all birds needed was seed, fresh water, grit, and a little lettuce, Dr. Lafeber believed that birds needed much, much more. He believed that birds needed a healthy, balanced diet consisting of seeds, vegetables, grains, fruit, some meat, and lots of fresh water. Pellets did not yet exist on the market, and even back then he was working hard to come up with a better alternative than seeds. We learned a great deal from Dr. Lafeber, and Charlie, who was lucky enough to receive the benefit of his knowledge, remains happy and healthy.

Over the years, my flock increased from 1 to more than 20. For more than 25 years, I have cooked for my birds, adjusting and improving the recipes I had. As more information became available—through sources such as bird clubs, the Internet, *Bird Talk* magazine, *Winged Wisdom*, and Sally Blanchard's *Pet Bird Report*, I continued learning what is best for our birds.

After cooking for my birds for all of these years, developing well-balanced recipes with the help of veterinarians, breeders, and other resources, and learning more and more about the importance of nutrition in a bird's diet, I decided to develop a cookbook for birds. The number-one health problem with today's birds is poor nutrition–in order to thrive and to live a long life, your bird needs a healthy and balanced diet. Where can birds get that balanced diet? Variety! Fresh vegetables, grains, fruits, and meat are all necessary components to a balanced diet. Yes, I said meat. Most parrots love to chew on a chicken bone, cracking it open to eat the marrow inside. Others enjoy a good steak.

It is sometimes difficult to provide birds with the properly balanced diets they need–today we know that each species has its own nutritional needs. Furthermore, not only does each species have different requirements, but individuals within each species may also have different nutritional needs. We know that African Greys need a diet that is higher in calcium, while Amazons and cockatiels need more vitamin A in their diets. Weaning birds require more protein because of fast-growing bodies. Breeding birds also have different nutritional needs. Because there are hundreds of species, pet food manufacturers can't afford to produce a food that meets not only a specific species' needs, but also meets the individual's needs within the species. It would be extremely costly.

True, there are now pellets on the market and they are excellent to feed your birds, but even they can't meet each and every species' needs. Plus, there are some species of birds, as well as individual birds, that need a much lower protein level than what in is the pellets. My cockatoo, Toby, loves pellets, but the protein in it was damaging her kidneys.

So what to do? This is where the cookbook for birds comes in. By picking and choosing a wide variety of different foods from the basic food groups, you can give your birds a much healthier diet. This book contains 150 recipes that are both nutritious and tasty. They have been tested on my birds and each bird has its favorites. So try them out. See which ones your bird enjoys or try using the basic recipe, experiment, add foods your bird likes, and omit the ones he does not enjoy.

Many of the recipes in this book were developed with the help of both veterinarians and bird breeders, who are well aware of how much a nutritious diet benefits the health of all birds. They were an enormous help and I have been using them as a source of information for over 25 years now. Other people contributed to my knowledge of birds and the importance of their nutrition as well. My avian veterinarian in Hillsboro was Dr. Dave Barno, who has helped my birds through the years. Not only did he answer all my questions, but he also kept me updated with new information. I also know several wonder breeders and bird lovers, such as Smiles and John Germeau, Don and Dorothy Smith, Joyce Bradford, Gudrun Maybaum, and Jack Devine from Macaw Landing Foundation. Numerous other wonderful people from several different bird clubs served as sources of information for this book.

This cookbook will serve as an invaluable resource for all bird owners concerned with the health and well-being of their birds.

Measurement
Conversion Chart

US to Metric

1/4 teaspoon = 1 milliliter (mL)
1/2 teaspoon = 2 mL
1 teaspoon = 5 mL
1 tablespoon = 15 mL

1 ounce (liquid) = 29.56 mL
1 ounce (dry) = 30 grams
1 pound (dry) = 454 grams

1/4 cup = 50 mL
1/3 cup = 75 mL
1/2 cup = 125 mL
2/3 cup = 150 mL
3/4 cup = 175 mL
1 cup = 250 mL

1 pint = 473 mL
1 quart = 946 mL
1 gallon = 3785.4

1 inch=2.54 centimeters
1 cm=10 millimeters
10 millimeters=0.3937 inches

Fahrenheit to Celsius

-10° F= -23° C (coldest area of freezer)
0° F= -17° C (freezer)

32° F= 0° C (water freezes)
115° F= 46° C (water simmers)
130° F= 54° C (water scalds)
212° F= 100° C (water boils)

234° F= 112° C (soft ball)
244° F= 117° C (firm ball)
250° F= 121° C (hard ball)

300° F= 149° C (low oven)
350° F= 177° C (moderate oven)
400° F= 204° C (hot oven)
450° F= 232°C (very hot oven)
500° F= 260° C (extremely hot oven)

How to convert Fahrenheit and Celcius temperatures

Celcius to Fahrenheit:

Multiply the Celcius temperature by 9.
Divide that answer by 5.
Then, add 32.

Fahrenheit to Celcius:

Subtract 32 from the Fahrenheit temperature.
Divide the answer by 9.
Then, multiply that answer by 5.

$$Celcius° = 5/9 \ (F° - 32°) \quad Fahrenheit° = 9/5 \ C° + 32°$$

Part One:

The Importance of a Balanced Diet

The Need for More Than Seed

Good nutrition is simply the best way to keep your bird healthy. Most problems that avian veterinarians see could have been prevented with proper nutrition. However, providing your bird with proper nutrition involves much more than feeding him only commercial seeds and pellets. In order to stay healthy, your companion bird needs a varied, well-balanced diet. Seeds and pellets can make up a bulk of this diet, but they are not enough by themselves.

Avian nutrition is a new field. Most of the research done on nutrition to develop the commercial pellet and seed diets has been done in the poultry industry. It is only recently that some research has been conducted for parrots and other companion birds. One study using budgies determined that a budgie who was fed an exclusive, seed-only diet lived on the average of 3-5 years. In the same study, budgies who were fed fruits, vegetables, grains, and healthy table foods lived 10-15 years. This is three times as long as those on an all-seed diet!

Furthermore, in the wild, parrots and other birds consume a wide variety of fruits, vegetables, and, yes, even meat. Similarly, our pet birds also need a varied, balanced diet to stay healthy. In addition, there are more than 350 different species of parrots alone, with more than 350 different nutritional needs. Nutritional needs vary, not only

Though pellets claim to complete your bird's dietary needs, pellets should only be a part of your bird's diet. A healthy amount is about 25 percent of your bird's daily diet.

between species, but between individuals as well. A diet that is 100 percent complete for one bird may not be complete for another bird. This is true in all animals. So how do we provide what each species needs?

We can meet these needs by providing variety. The wider range of variety, the better. That is why the recipes in this book are so important. These are healthy recipes of all types of food, and when served in variation, they offer a more nutritious, well-balanced alternative to seed-only and pellet-only diets. For all of our birds, I feed 25 percent pellets, 25 percent seeds, 5 percent nuts, and 45 percent other healthy foods, using the recipes found in this book.

It is also important to remember that parrots and other birds can be picky. They have their likes and dislikes, just as humans do. Therefore, with 150 different healthy recipes to choose from, your birds are certain to find various foods that will strike their fancy. Furthermore, you do not have to spend money on vitamins or mineral supplements because your birds will be receiving these vitamins and minerals in the foods they are eating. (Always check with your avian veterinarian if your particular bird still requires these additives.)

The following is a good ratio to use for providing a well-balanced diet for your bird through seeds, pellets, and healthy foods.
25% pellets
25% seeds
45% healthy foods
5% nuts

Pellet Diets

Recently, pelleted diets have become very popular. Some manufacturers claim that they are 100 percent complete. Unfortunately, a few manufacturers also state that a pelleted diet is the only thing that the bird requires and that there is no need to supplement with vegetables, fruits, or healthy table foods. It is true that a pelleted diet does contain vitamins and minerals, but they are added prior to the heating process and can be destroyed by the heat.

Therefore, if you are feeding a pelleted diet, you still need to supplement with other foods, though vitamin and mineral supplements may not necessarily be needed. Check with your avian veterinarian to see if you should be adding any vitamins and minerals.

Because pellets are relatively new on the market, not enough research has been done on the long-term effects of a pellet-only diet. Even the manufacturers can't agree on which method of making pellets is the best. A few veterinarians have reported kidney problems as well as other systemic problems that have been associated with a pellet-only diet.

It should be noted that when a bird is on a pellet diet, the droppings may be bulkier and also change color. If you are converting your bird over to a pelleted diet, be aware of this. It should not unnecessarily alarm you into thinking that something is wrong with your bird. You should still monitor the droppings for any other changes. As always, if you are in doubt, check with your avian veterinarian.

Methods of Processing Pellets

Pellets are processed one of two ways. The first method is the pelleted, or compression, method. The second way is the extrusion, or expansion, method. The end results look different and feel different as well. Many companies add natural food colorings to their pellets. This is mainly for the owners, but remember that birds can distinguish colors as well as textures. Some manufacturers may even add different flavors to make it more appetizing.

Pelleted Method

In the pelleted or compression method, the ingredients used are finely ground up and vitamins and minerals are added. This material is then heated by steam to about 180°F. This mix is forced through a die and compressed into a pellet. The starch and protein in the ground-up material become sticky when heated by steam, allowing the once-dry mix to be compressed, holding the pellet together. Any fine powder that remains is removed during the cooling process when the pellets are moved across a screen.

The nutritional loss is little because the heat level is low. Even though this process does kill off some bacteria, there can still be some present. This will include both the bad bacteria as well as the good bacteria. This method results in a denser, heavier pellet.

Pellets can be a part of your bird's diet—just be sure that you include other healthy foods as well.

In the pelleted method, the end results contain less fat and may have lower caloric densities. This means that the bird may eat as much as 20 to 30 percent more pelleted foods than the extruded foods.

Extruded Method

In the extruded or expansion method, the ingredients are also finely ground up. Vitamins and minerals are added. These ingredients are then mixed with water and cooked under pressure at temperatures over 300°F. A gruel is formed. This gruel is then forced through a die.

When the gruel hits the air, it expands to form a pellet. These pellets can be different shapes as well as colors. Dyes are added at the time that the gruel is forced through the die. Though uniform in size, it is less dense and lighter than the compressed or pelleted method. Because the temperature is higher, it kills off any bacteria that may be

One type of shape, size, and color pellet does not provide interesting variety for the bird.

present. However, these higher temperatures can also destroy some of the vitamins and minerals. The manufacturers of this form of pellets feel that cooking at the higher temperatures will cause the fiber present to become more digestible. Other manufacturers feel that this causes a lower fiber diet.

Because the extruded diets are more concentrated, the bird will eat less. They do cost more than the pelleted diets. However, because birds eat less to maintain their requirements, it balances out.

Pellet Varieties

Pellets come in a variety of different shapes, sizes, textures, tastes, and colors. Some will even have a pleasant, fruity smell while others seem to have little to no aroma at all. Some very brave friends of mine have actually tasted these pellets. They said they had a fruity taste.

For smaller birds, pellets are smaller or appear like crumbles. To make these crumbles, the pellets are crushed into very small pieces.

Things to Know About Pellets

Keep the following tips when feeding pellets to your birds to avoid problems and to allow your bird to get the most out of eating them.

- The denser the product, the less it crumbles when a bird bites into it.
- Read the label! Avoid pellet diets that contain animal by-products because these can spoil or develop gram-negative bacteria. These diets need to be chemically contained, using artificial ingredients.
- Those that use high-quality vegetable protein reduce the possibility of bacterial contamination.
- Smell the pellets once you open them to make sure that they smell fresh. The odor should be pleasant. It should not smell rancid.
- Pellets are often made into interesting shapes and colors, which attract birds.

- Pellets may also contain spirulina, kelp meal, human-grade whole dried eggs, brewer's yeast, and natural fruit flavoring. All-natural diets are more expensive, using natural preservatives to increase shelf life. Pellets can also be fortified with Lactobacillis acidophilis, which helps maintain healthy intestinal conditions. They may also contain yucca extract, which helps reduce gases and odors.

- Storage should be in a dark, dry, cool place, such as in the refrigerator.

- What to do with the leftover powder? Try sprinkling it on top of the bird's soft food.

- Do not feed supplementary vitamins and minerals to your birds if they are on a pellet diet. You should also avoid feeding cuttlebones, mineral blocks, and oyster shell. Meat products, eggs, cheese, and nuts must be restricted.

- Most pellet diets have allowed for 10 to 20 percent added fruit and vegetables. For the occasional snack, table food is also allowed, but in very limited amounts.

Pellet Pros and Cons

Advantages

Vitamins and minerals are already added in the pellets

Provides more protein than seeds can provide

No seed moths

Less waste

Less mess with some birds

Some have different shapes and colors

Cost less than seed per serving

Disadvantages

Some avian veterinarians have reported vitamin toxicity in some individuals

Protein can be too high and can cause kidney problems

Proper storage still necessary

Some birds will not eat the pellets

Birds may enjoy throwing the pellets

Seed Mixes

There are many different types of seed mixes on the market today. Choosing a good seed mix can be very confusing, even to the experienced bird owner. There are good and bad seed mixes available. Seeds have some, but not enough, nutritional value.

They are mostly empty calories. In effect, it is the ultimate junk food for birds! Seed mixes need to have healthy table foods, veggies, fruits, etc., added to them to meet the bird's nutritional needs.

Bad Mixes vs. Good Mixes

How do you choose a good seed mix rather than a bad seed mix? Look at it! A good seed mix contains little or no sunflower seeds. It should look clean, without bugs or webbing. It should contain a variety of seeds. Some of the better seed mixes contain pellets, dehydrated fruit, and vegetables. The package should be labeled accurately as to the contents. It should also have a guaranteed analysis on the label.

Choosing the Right Type of Seed Mix

The type of seed mix that you purchase will depend on the type of bird you own. Large hookbill mixes are not appropriate for smaller hookbills. Large hookbills can crack the hulls of larger seeds and nuts, whereas the small hookbills cannot. There will

Seeds are acceptable as a small portion of your bird's daily diet, but a bird needs much more than seeds to stay healthy.

Old seed can be dangerous to your bird—feed only fresh seeds and change the seeds often.

be more wasted seed if you attempt to feed a small hookbill diet to a large hookbill, and the bird will lose weight as a result. You can purchase unsalted nuts and add them to the seed mix if you feel your bird needs them or use them as a special treat. However, do not add too many nuts, because of their high fat content.

Avoiding Seed Contamination

The package should be whole and intact. A ripped, torn, or opened package may contain seed moths, other bugs, or even rodent droppings. Seed moths, by themselves, are not dangerous to your bird. Live moths are an indication that there are no harmful contaminants in the seed mix. In fact, seed moths are another source of protein for your bird. However, if you object to the presence of seed moths in your house, you can easily kill them by freezing your seed mix for 48 hours or by microwaving it.

Old seed can be dangerous to your bird because the seeds and nuts can go rancid and become toxic. Feed only fresh seeds. Seeds that germinate are fresh seeds and will provide nutrients for your bird.

Contamination can occur at any time. It can occur during the growing, harvesting, and packaging of the seed. It can occur during the transportation, delivery, and selling of the seed. The seed package does not need to have been opened for contamination to have occurred. The contamination may have happened before the seeds were packaged and can be in the form of pesticides, bacteria, rodent droppings, or bugs.

Sterilizing Seeds

To eliminate contamination caused by bacteria and bugs, you can microwave your seed. Follow this procedure: Place the seed in a 9x11 inch microwaveable glass pan.

The seeds should be no more than an inch deep. Microwave the seed on high for two minutes. Stir the seed well. Then microwave two minutes more. With a clean utensil, stir the seed again. Microwave the seed

No seed mix alone is an adequate diet for any bird!

once more for another two minutes. Once again, stir with a clean utensil and let cool. It is important to use a clean spoon each time you stir so that you do not recontaminate the seed. Total microwave time is six minutes. After the seed has cooled, refrigerate it in an airtight plastic container (not in a coffee can).

NOTE: Many people who tried this have reported that it creates a rather strong odor. In other words, it stinks. Best to do on nice days when you can open your windows.

Changing the Seeds

Another problem with seed diets is the hulls that remain behind. Many birds have starved to death because owners thought that there were still seeds left in their food cups. Instead it was actually just empty seed hulls. To avoid this situation, change the seed daily. You can tell how much your bird has eaten because the seed hulls can easily be blown off the top of the cup.

How to Get Your Bird to Eat a Balanced Diet

Some birds are picky or reluctant to try new foods. However, the following tips may help you get your bird to eat the balanced diet he needs.

Sweetening

Sometimes sweetening the food with a little honey may prompt nibbling. However, you must be careful about making this a habit. Too many sweets are not good for birds (or humans). It could even lead to diabetes or death.

Millet is a favorite seed of many birds. This is like candy to them. Try sprinkling millet or pieces of millet spray on top of the food. Start with more millet than the other healthy food. Push the millet down into the new food. Your bird will pick at the millet and maybe even get a taste of the other food. As the bird starts to do this more readily, decrease the amount of millet until you no longer have to add any. I call this the sneaky approach. (With humans, moms may add sauces to veggies to get their kids to taste them.)

Birds are flock creatures and usually eat better in a social setting, either with you and your family or other birds.

Offering Freshly Sprouted Seeds

You can also try offering freshly sprouted seeds. You can start growing seeds yourself or buy sprouts in the produce section of your local grocery store. Varieties include alfalfa, beans, and mixtures with radish and clover. This is a special treat for most birds and will start them getting used to different foods. Freshly sprouted seeds also contain lots of vitamins and minerals. Freshly sprouted wheat grass is also a real treat.

Alternating

Another method that may work is to alternate offering seed a few hours at a time, then offering fresh fruits and vegetables or other healthy foods for a few hours. Keep track of your bird's weight if you do this. Remember to offer the fruits, veggies, etc., first, because your bird will be the hungriest in the morning. He will be more likely to try new foods then.

Members of the Flock

Keep in mind that birds are flock creatures. This means that they will eat better in a social setting. If you have a finicky eater or you are just introducing a new food to the bird, try eating the food yourself with the bird watching.

If you or any other birds you own are eating with gusto, your finicky eater will be much more likely to eat or taste the food as well. Some birds need to be right next to you when you try this.

Familiar Surroundings

Birds eat better in familiar surroundings, without distractions. A noisy, chaotic environment will disrupt your bird's mealtime (and may give you ulcers as well). Try a nice quiet environment while you eat.

Birds eat better in familiar surroundings and in a quiet environment.

Be Persistent

Keep offering the food—don't give up! Dietary changes can be accomplished with much patience and persistence on the part of the owner. Just because you offered the food two or three times and the bird refused to eat it doesn't mean that you should give up. It may take months before you see your bird enjoying all those wonderful foods that you are slaving away to prepare. Too many people only offer a new food once or twice and stop offering it. Birds are like children—they may take a while before they will try something new.

Offer Special Goodies

Another way to get birds to try new foods is by offering special goodies or treats. I feed my birds all types of goodies. Mix other healthy foods in with their special treats.

For special treats, try stringing grapes, popcorn, and/or certain cereals on thin

One way to get your bird to eat different kinds of healthy foods is to offer foods with a fun, new presentation.

string. Remove as soon as the food disappears. Pine cones stuffed with peanut butter and seeds are welcomed by the larger birds.

Offer Different Presentations

Sometimes presenting the food differently will get the bird to eat. Try chopping the food up into small pieces or shredding it. Alternate different foods on a daily basis. On the market is a birdie "shish-kabob" toy made to hold food. While the bird plays with the toy, he is nibbling at the food at the same time.

Use Jealousy to Your Advantage

Don't forget about the power of jealousy. Whenever you have more than one bird, there is a competition for your attention. Use it to encourage your birds to do what you want them to do. (HINT: This advice pertains to other areas of training as well.) Birds are very much like little children. Whatever one has, the other one wants.

Make It a Family Affair

Make eating a family affair—get your bird involved. Your bird will be the healthier for it. This is not meant to imply that you should allow your bird to walk over your food or go from plate to plate, taking whatever he/she wants. Little birdie footprints in your mashed potatoes are not exactly appetizing. Birds must learn proper table manners.

Try using his own dish or make a special place for him by placing his stand near the table. A bird without table manners is open to many different accidents, such as being scalded from hot foods or eating foods that may be harmful to him.

Things to Remember Before You Start

The following section lists many important tips you should take into consideration before you begin cooking for your birds.

- Not all ovens are created equal. Cooking times may vary greatly. My double ovens cook differently—the top cooks faster than the bottom one, and my full-size oven cooks even faster. When you are cooking, check on the food often. Use the toothpick test to see if it is done.

- When cooking for your birds, always use human-grade ingredients. The best source for many of these ingredients is at a health food store. Birds do not need the additives and preservatives that go into so many of our foods.

- Never cook using nonstick cookware if your bird lives in the house. Heated, nonstick cookware has a special coating, and this coating emits a colorless, odorless fume when heated that kills birds almost immediately. It was originally thought that only burned or overheated nonstick cookware emitted these dangerous fumes, but it was recently discovered that this cookware could kill birds even at normal cooking temperatures. Nonstick coating can be found on griddles, pans, deep fryers, bread makers, crock pots, and many other kitchen utensils and appliances. To be safe, only use cookware made of stainless steel, copper, or other materials that do not have nonstick coating present.

- Fresh foods are healthier than frozen food. Frozen foods are available year round where some fresh produce may not be available. During the summer, I grow my own vegetables and fruits. I do not spray my produce with insecticides or use any unnatural chemicals. During the winter, I try to buy organic produce.

- Check the ingredients on cans, boxes, and bags. Buy low-sodium and low or sugar-free items instead of those loaded with salt or sugar.

- Always thoroughly wash any fruits or vegetables you buy.

- Note also that, like people, birds can develop food allergies. These include but are not limited to peanut allergies, sulfur allergies, and even spirulina allergies.

- Sulfites are found on dried fruits. This helps to preserve them for a longer shelf life. I dry my own fruits and vegetables. I have found it cheaper and healthier, not only for my birds, but for my entire family.

- I have recently read about spirulina causing aggressive behavior, especially in some cockatoos. If your bird exhibits any problems from spirulina, try using wheat grass instead.

- Remove any wet foods after 1-2 hours, sooner in warmer temperatures. Egg products are a great breeding ground for bacteria, and should be removed after 1 hour. Breads can be left for 3-5 hours.

- Always provide lots of fresh, clean water. Give your birds a good seed mix or pellet mix, ones that do not use dyes or ones that contain fruits and vegetables preserved with sulfites. Natural is the best way to go.

- Some birds need more calcium, like Greys, or more vitamin A, like Amazons. If you are cooking for these birds, try scraping a mineral block to add more calcium, or using foods that have higher amounts of vitamin A.

- Experiment with your own recipes. Add or subtract ingredients according to your bird's likes and dislikes. Many of the recipes in this book began that very way. All of the recipes in this book have been bird tested and approved. So go ahead and experiment. Getting your bird to eat a healthy diet doesn't have to be difficult. These recipes will help you do that.

The Food Groups

Birds, like people, need to have a variety of foods that come from the different food groups. The following is a general overview of the basic food groups and what types of foods in these groups are healthy for your bird. Many of the foods listed in these various food groups are used in the recipes of this book.

Grains

Most breads and grain products are good sources of niacin, thiamin, phosphorus, potassium, and sometimes iron. Yeast contains vitamin B6 and folacin.

Breads and muffins are easy to cook and you can hide all kinds of things in there that are good for your bird. In fact, even the pickiest bird will peck at muffins and breads. I use muffins to hide vegetables, and even vitamins, minerals and other supplements that my birds would normally not touch.

Grains you can feed your bird include the following foods:

- Breads, whole-wheat bread, multi-grain breads, etc. (Whole-grain breads are a good source of B6, E, magnesium, and zinc.)
- Pancakes, waffles, crepes, etc.
- Cooked rice, preferably brown, but white is okay
- Wheat berries
- Pearl barley

- Triticale
- Noodles, pasta (including spaghetti, ravioli, macaroni, etc.)
- Oatmeal, Cream of Wheat, or Cream of Rice
- Low-salt pretzels, low-salt crackers, or melba toast
- Wheat, flour, or flavored tortillas
- Matzoh, matzoh meal, cake meal
- Buckwheat
- Bagels
- Low-sugar cereals, such as Cheerios, Life, Chex, Kix, Berry Kix, etc.
- Grains, such as whole-wheat flour, corn flour, rye flour, white flour, rice flour, multigrain flour, etc.

Vegetables

Vegetables are extremely important sources of vitamins and minerals. They should be thoroughly washed before you give them to your bird to remove any chemicals that might be on the skins. You can serve them fresh, steamed, baked in a sauce such as tomato sauce, or boiled. Frozen vegetables are also acceptable. (Thaw and heat them before serving.)

The following vegetables are all suitable for your bird.

- Alfalfa sprouts (leaves). Alfalfa is rich in calcium, magnesium, potassium, and carotene and acts as an appetite stimulant.
- Artichokes
- Asparagus (especially tips). This is a good source of vitamin A and niacin.
- Baby corn
- Bamboo shoots. These are of little nutritional value; feed only once in a while.
- Canned bamboo shoots. High in sodium.
- Beans (pinto, kidney, navy, garbanzo, mung, butter, haricot, adzuki, soy, etc., cooked.) Most are high in various vitamins and minerals.
- Beans (pole, wax, green, etc.)
- Beets. Beet greens are very high in vitamin A, potassium, thiamin, and riboflavin.
- Bok choy
- Broccoli. Broccoli is a good source of vitamin A, riboflavin, and ascorbic acid.
- Brocciflower (combination of broccoli and cauliflower)
- Brussels sprouts. Feed in moderation; it can cause thyroid problems if overfed.

This is a good source of potassium, thiamin, and ascorbic acid.

Vegetables, such as corn, are extremely important sources of vitamins and minerals and are a necessary part of your bird's diet.

- Cabbage (dark green; red cabbage lower in vitamin content)
- Carrots (baby, raw, tops included or cooked). Carrots help to promote tissue healing and are a source of vitamin A and potassium
- Cauliflower. This is a good source of potassium.
- Cayenne (or capsicum). This is a digestive aid and a good source of vitamins A, C, B-complex, calcium, phosphorous, and iron. Anti-inflammatory.
- Celery. This is of little nutritional value, so feed once in a while only. It has a high water content.
- Chard
- Chayote
- Chicory (vitamin A)
- Chickweed. This is high in vitamin A, and it strengthens the stomach and bowels.
- Chili peppers (high in vitamin A)
- Cilantro
- Collard greens. These are a good source of calcium, vitamins A and C, potassium, and riboflavin.
- Corn on the cob (fresh or cooked)
- Comfrey
- Cucumbers (high water content)
- Dandelion greens (rich in vitamin A)
- Eggplant (cooked, mature ripe pods only)
- Endive (source of vitamin A)
- Garlic. This has anti-tumor properties, contains 18 anti-viral, anti-fungal, and anti-bacterial substances. A natural antibiotic, it stimulates the immune system and kills parasites. It also helps to eliminate lead, zinc, and other toxins.

- Ginger root. This is used for motion sickness when made into "tea." Soak three slices of fresh ginger root in water for 15 minutes. Good in vegetable mixes, but not used alone.
- Green beans (source of vitamin A and potassium)
- Indian corn
- Jicama
- Kale (vitamin A)
- Kohrabi
- Leeks
- Lettuce. Feed in moderation because of its high water content. Romaine, chickory, Boston, aruula, and other dark or red varieties are better than iceberg and other light greens. Some varieties are a source of thiamin and vitamin A, though in small amounts.
- Lima beans. Baby lima beans are a good source of potassium, thiamin, and niacin.
- Mixed veggies (canned). This is a high vitamin A source but also may contain high amounts of sodium.
- Mixed veggies (frozen). This is a good source of vitamin A, though not as high as in the canned varieties, but lower in sodium.
- Mushrooms. Even though they contain niacin and riboflavin, they have little nutritional value. Canned mushrooms have a high sodium value. I serve these cooked in some dishes, but I use them very sparingly.
- Mustard greens (vitamin A and calcium)
- Okra
- Onions. These are questionable. There are two schools of thought about onions. Some people say that a little onion is okay; others say they don't ever use it. Onions, like some other oxalates, can bind up calcium. I use it in many of the dishes that I make for my birds but only as a seasoning.
- Parsley. This is high in vitamins A and C, as well as calcium, chlorine, copper, phosporus, potassium, and an incomplete protein. It helps to cleanse the kidneys.
- Peas (green, sugar snap, peas in pods, etc.)
- Peas (green and yellow split). Peas are a good source of vitamin A, phosphorus, thiamin, and niacin.

- Peppers (red, green, yellow, jalapeno, chili, etc.) Red pepper flakes are high in vitamins A and C, as well as several minerals. They help increase circulation and promote clotting.

- Potatoes (white, red, new, cooked). Baked is best. White and red potatoes are good sources of B6, potassium, phosphorus, iron, thiamin, niacin, and ascorbic acid.

- Pumpkin (cooked). The seeds are gland healers, and they may kill some intestinal parasites. The high zinc content promotes tissue growth. Canned pumpkin contains the highest amount of vitamin A of all vegetables.

- Radishes (little nutritional value)

- Snow peas

- Spinach. Feed in moderation because it can bind calcium in system, leading to hypocalcemia. It is high in vitamin A and potassium. Frozen cooked spinach has the highest amount.

- Sprouts (alfalfa, bean, etc.). These contain vitamin C and are nourishing to the glands but an incomplete protein.

- Squash (butternut, acorn etc., cooked). This is a good source of vitamin A, potassium, and niacin. Summer squash has lower vitamin value than winter varieties do. Seeds high in silenium.

- Sweet potatoes. This is a good source of vitamin A, niacin, and B6. Boiled is best. Canned mashed sweet potatoes are highest in vitamin value, though not the candied variety.

- Tomatoes. This is a source of vitamin A and ascorbic acid. Tomato paste, sauce, and puree all have high vitamin A values but may also be high in sodium.

- Turnip greens. Turnip greens are high in vitamin A and calcium.

- Watercress. This is high in vitamins A, C, and E, and aids the kidneys.

- Yams (good source of vitamin A, niacin, and B6). Boiled is best.

- Yellow wax beans (lower vitamin value than green beans)

- Zucchini (see squash)

Fruits

Fruits are a favorite of most birds, while other birds won't touch them. They provide many important vitamins which are vital to a bird's health. High in water content, your bird's droppings may become watery as well. Some birds who are receiving a lot of fruit may not be drinking as much. This is not necessarily a cause to be alarmed. Birds do not eat the skins of fruits; instead, they like to fling them all over the place. Save yourself some of this mess by peeling some of these fruits for them first. Seeds will need to be removed before serving.

- Apples (all varieties, no seeds, including applesauce). Apples contain malic and tartaric acids, which keep the liver and digestion healthy.
- Apricots (no pits or area near pit). Dried, unsweetened apricots have the highest vitamin A content of all fruits. Apricots are also and excellent source of potassium, niacin, riboflavin and iron.
- Bananas (good source of B6, potassium, and riboflavin). Remove peel before giving it to your bird.
- Berries (strawberries, blueberries, blackberries, raspberries, cranberries, etc.). Strawberry leaves help to remove metallic poisons from the blood. Raspberry leaves help soothe the entire system. Blackberries are a source of ascorbic acid, and strawberries a source of vitamin C and potassium.
- Cactus fruit
- Chermoya
- Cherries, no pits
- Coconuts
- Coquitos (mini coconuts)
- Currants
- Dates (source of potassium and niacin)
- Figs (source of potassium and iron)
- Grapes (red, green, black, etc.) Grapes help the kidneys by decreasing the acidity of uric acid.
- Grapefruit (source of vitamin C)
- Guavas
- Kiwis (source of potassium and ascorbic acid)
- Kumquats
- Leechees
- Lemons
- Mangos (source of vitamin A, niacin, vitamin C, and potassium)
- Melons (rinds are toxic; watermelon, honeydew, crenshaw, cantaloupe, casaba, Santa Claus, Juan, Canary Island, etc.). Cantaloupe is a good source for vitamin A, C, and potassium. Watermelon, while high in water content, contains vitamins

A, C, potassium, thiamin, and phosphorus. Honeydew is low in vitamin content.

- Nectarines (no pits or area near pit). This is a source of vitamin A and niacin.
- Oranges. This is a good source of vitamin C. Frozen, undiluted concentrate can be used for cooking and contains the highest amount of potassium and vitamin C.
- Papaya. Papaya contains papain, which aids digestion and helps the stomach and pancreas, and it is high in vitamin C.

Papaya is a particularly good fruit for birds, aiding in digestion and helping the stomach and pancreas. Just make sure to remove the seeds.

- Passionfruit
- Peaches (no pits or area near pit). Unsweetened, dried varieties have more vitamin A, riboflavin, and potassium.
- Pears (no seeds). This is a source of potassium.
- Pepino Melons
- Pineapple
- Plantains. Plantains are a source of vitamins A and C and potassium.
- Plums (no pits)
- Pomegranates. These are great for the kidneys.
- Raisins. These are a source of potassium, thiamin, niacin, and phosphorus.
- Starfruit
- Tangerines

Dairy Group

Many parrots are not receiving enough calcium in their diets because owners do not give their birds any foods from this group. As with people, calcium is very important. Remember that too much cheese can cause constipation. Birds will also have a problem in digesting milk. Use only sparingly or as dried milk in cooking.

- Cottage cheese
- Yogurt. This is a good source of calcium, potassium, and phosphorus.
- Eggs (any style, shells included). Eggs are asource of B12, and the yolks are a good source of vitamin D, but eggs are high in cholesterol.
- Milk (used as dried in cooking). Milk is a source of vitamins D, B12, and magnesium.)
- Cheese (any variety is acceptable). Birds love their cheese mixed with other foods, such as in macaroni and pizza. These cheeses include cheddar, mozzarella, Muenster, provolone, Swiss, American, and parmesan. Cheddar has the highest cholesterol values and calories, Swiss the most calcium, parmesan the greatest amounts of phosphorus and sodium, and muenster and cheddar the highest fat content.

Meat Group

Birds need protein, and a seed diet, unfortunately, provides little protein. In the wild birds, have been observed eating insects. Protein sources should be used in moderation. Meat and poultry are good sources of B12, B6, and zinc.

- Steak (no pink showing). The vitamin values vary slightly between different cuts, but there is a large difference in fat and in calories.
- Roast beef (vitamin value varies between cuts)
- Turkey. While turkey is a good source of zinc, different parts of the turkey will vary in fat and calories.
- Chicken. While it is a good source of zinc, like turkey, different parts of the chicken will vary in fat and calories. When feeding your bird chicken or turkey, you can give the wing tips, thigh bones, and wing bones (depending on the size of your bird) with some meat on them. The bird will crack the bone open and eat the marrow inside.
- Tuna fish (water packed; make sure it is low in sodium as well)
- Liver, cooked (contains extremely high values of vitamin A and also contains B12, B6, D, and folacin)
- Ribs (okay on occasions). Large birds, especially, love ribs and crack the bones open to get the marrow. Make sure they are thoroughly cooked.
- Fish (some types of non-oily, well-cooked fish may be acceptable). Fish is an excellent source of protein, but make sure it is thoroughly cooked and has no bones.

🍲 Lamb. While I almost never see it listed, I have given my birds lamb chops whenever we have them. I also talked to my avian veterinarian and he sees no problems with it either.

Nuts

Except for acorns, birds love all kinds of nuts. They have different degrees of fat content, so use moderation when supplementing with nuts and also make sure they are unsalted. Remember that certain nuts such as pecans are polished nuts, which contain dyes. If you can find unpolished nuts, these are much better for your bird. They are hard to find and do not look very pretty, but they are worth the search. Nuts are also a good source of phosphorus, potassium, vitamin A, zinc, biotin, riboflavin, selenium, copper, niacin, and (in some nuts) folic acid.

❧ Almonds (high in calcium and B6, which helps fight infections; also a good source of phosphorus and potassium.) Almonds contain the highest amount of calcium in all nuts, and the second-largest amount of potassium and phosphorus.

❧ Brazil nuts (contain the highest source of phosphorus of all nuts and also high in potassium; not as high in fat as macadamia nuts). These nuts are loved by macaws, especially hyacinth macaws.

Birds love nuts, and most contain necessary vitamins and minerals, such as potassium, phosphorus, Vitamin A, and Vitamin E.

- Cashew nuts (low in fat)
- Filberts (or hazelnuts). These nuts have the second-highest amount in calcium and contain some vitamin A.
- Macadamia nuts (highest in fat and calorie content of all nuts and also low in protein)
- Peanuts (contain the highest amount of protein of all nuts; a good source of vitamin E)
- Pecans (low in protein, but high in calories). This nut has some vitamin A value and a little calcium.
- Pine nuts (contain the lowest amount of calcium of all nuts; also is low in protein and in phosphorus)
- Pistachio nuts (contains the highest amount of potassium and vitamin A of all nuts; has the third-highest phosphorus value). These nuts also contain calcium, thiamin, and phosphorus.
- Walnuts (has some vitamin A value and is the fourth-highest in potassium)
- Almond butter, cashew butter, hazelnut butter, peanut butter, and macadamia butter (homemade is best because you can cut down on the oil and sugar used)

Fats and Oils

These should be used sparingly. When possible, you can use nonstick spray.

- Margarine (contains the same amount of calories as butter, but it has no cholesterol. Some, however, have sodium added to them. It also contains vitamins A and E.)
- Butter (same calories as margarine, but contains cholesterol)
- Oils (include corn, olive, peanut, safflower, soybean and sunflower oils). Calorie content is the same for all oils, although slightly higher than that of margarine or butter, but it has no cholesterol. Has calcium, phosphorus, sodium, vitamin A, thiamin, riboflavin, niacin, ascorbic acid, and vitamin E values.

Many birds love peppers and other foods that taste spicy-hot to humans.

Seasonings and Flavorings

With some exceptions, such as chili powder and paprika, most seasonings offer little to no nutritional value, usually containing a trace amount of vitamins and minerals at most. Seasonings and flavorings should be used sparingly. If using fresh herbs, make sure they are thoroughly washed first. You won't need to use as much, either.

- Salt (good source of iodine; should be used sparingly)
- Yeast (a good source of B6 and folacin)
- Red chili peppers. These peppers make things spicy-hot for humans, but birds seem to enjoy it. Try the dried peppers on popcorn.

Vitamins, Minerals, and Amino Acids

A vitamin is an organic compound that is considered to be metabolically essential in small amounts in animal tissues. In simpler terms, it's an important but tiny ingredient in the diets of animals and humans. Usually obtained from food, vitamins are critical to good health.

Always check with your veterinarian before supplementing any of the vitamins, minerals, or amino acids outlined in this chapter. There are hundreds of species of birds, not counting subspecies, and then, as with humans, individual birds may require different amounts.

Furthermore, by giving your bird a varied, well-balanced diet using various recipes like the ones in this book, you usually will not have to worry about your bird having any vitamin, mineral, or amino acid deficiency. Birds on a seed-only diet do, however, have to worry about this problem. Consult your veterinarian to discuss these needs and whether your bird needs any vitamin supplements.

There are two main types of vitamins: fat-soluble and water-soluble.

Fat-Soluble Vitamins

Fat-soluble vitamins are found in fatty compounds and are carried in the body by fats. These vitamins are not soluble in water but are normally found in dissolved fats and are stored in the body.

Vitamin deficiencies can cause many different problems. However, before you go out and buy vitamins to give to your bird, you should also know that you can cause vitamin toxicity by giving too much of a certain vitamin. Consult your veterinarian before giving him vitamins.

And remember—the best way to ensure that your bird is receiving the amounts he needs from the start is to to give him a healthy, varied diet using the recipes in this book.

Vitamin A (Beta Carotene)

Function: Vitamin A is stored in the liver and is needed for good vision. Without adequate vitamin A, night vision is the first to be affected. It is essential for resistance to infections, particularly in the sinuses. This is one of the most common deficiencies in birds. It belongs to the group of vitamins that are known as carotenoids. It is important for healthy eyes, skin, and mucous membranes.

Symptoms of a Deficiency: A bird with a vitamin A deficiency lacks energy. The bird can have abnormal feather structure, coloring, and growth. Decreased egg production, longer time between clutches, and poor hatchability are also reported. Males will develop a low sperm count. In extreme cases, the central nervous system is affected. Sometimes there can be lesions around the

Vitamin A deficiencies are one of the most common in birds, so feed your avian companion plenty of yellow or green vegetables, such as broccoli.

eyes, mouth, feet, and skin. Bones may not develop properly, and even kidney problems may occur. Night blindness is also reported, as well as changes in the cornea. Skin problems evidenced by a dried, thickened appearance, can be seen on the feet, cere, and face. Swelling of the sublingual salivary gland can be present, especially in Amazons, African Greys, and Cockatoos. Renal gout may occur in some cases.

Symptoms of Toxicity: Decrease in appetite, weight loss, muscle soreness, enlarged liver and spleen, dermatitis, poor growth, diarrhea, and nausea.

Found: Vitamin A is found in most fruits, and in yellow or green vegetables. These foods include: beef, liver, carrots, squash, pumpkin, sweet potatoes, spinach, apricots, cantaloupe, dandelion leaves, red chili peppers, broccoli, peaches, egg yolk, and peas.

Vitamin D

Function: Vitamin D regulates the absorption of calcium from the intestines. Without enough vitamin D, the absorption of calcium is slowed, which can cause inadequate bone development. This can lead to rickets or fragile bones. It is stored in the bird's liver in limited amounts.

Symptoms of a Deficiency: Vitamin D deficiencies can result in a lack of energy, slow growth and bad feathers, poor egg production, egg binding, leg weakness, paralysis, and tremors, as well as skeletal deformities. Next to vitamin A, it is the second-most common vitamin deficiency reported.

Symptoms of Toxicity: Calcium deposits in heart, kidneys, joints, arteries, and other tissues.

Found: Vitamin D is also called the sunlight vitamin because it is produced in the skin by ultraviolet rays from the sun. Vitamin D3 is the only D vitamin that birds can use, unlike mammals. Foods that have vitamin D include fortified milk, egg yolks, some cereals, beef liver, and cheese. Cod liver oil is another source.

Vitamin E

Function: There are eight forms of vitamin E found in plants. Vitamin E is an antioxidant, which is used by the body to prevent chemicals in the body from damaging cells. Vitamin E deficiencies can lead to muscular dystrophy and other disorders. It is sometimes referred to as the sex vitamin. This is because it is necessary for the pituitary, adrenal, and sex hormones. Vitamin E works together with other minerals, especially selenium.

Vitamin K ensures proper blood clotting and liver function—it can be found predominantly in green vegetables.

Symptoms of a Deficiency: Birds with a vitamin E deficiency will lack vigor, develop problems that are associated with the nervous system, and develop blood and vascular disorders, anemia, and muscular disorders. Brain dysfunction and infertility have also been observed. In male birds, it can cause sterility if the deficiency is long term.

Symptoms of Toxicity: Vitamin E acts as an antagonist to vitamin A, destroying its antioxidant effects.

Found: Vitamin E is found in whole grains, some cereals, and fresh, leafy-green vegetables, such as spinach. It can be found in safflower oil, canned peaches, dried prunes, asparagus, broccoli, sweet potatoes, sunflower seeds, walnuts, almonds, brussel sprouts, and whole-grain breads. Feeding too much cod liver oil (to make up for vitamin D3) will lead to deficiencies because it will oxidize the vitamin E in the bird's system.

Water-Soluble Vitamins

The other type of vitamin is water-soluble. These are not stored in the body but are washed away with water, so they must be replenished continually.

Vitamin K

Function: Vitamin K ensures proper blood clotting through the manufacture of prothrombin (the factor in blood that causes clotting). Synthesis occurs in the intestines. This is true in both mammals and birds. Vitamin K is vital for proper liver function. Most diets have adequate vitamin K.

Symptoms of a Deficiency: A deficiency in vitamin K can cause a bird to bleed to death. Anemia, as well as blood and vascular disorders, can occur due to vitamin K deficiency. Deficiencies can also result from prolonged antibiotic use.

Symptoms of Toxicity: Not reported in birds, but in humans it can cause brain damage and red blood cell breakdown.

Found: Vitamin K is found predominantly in green vegetables, including broccoli, cabbage, asparagus, peas, green beans, turnip greens, spinach, and cheese. It is also produced by bacteria in the bowels.

Thiamin (B1)

Function: Thiamin, also known as B1, helps to maintain a healthy nervous system. The B vitamins are important in reproduction.

Symptoms of a Deficiency: Deficiencies in B1 can cause the nervous system to become inflamed, resulting in leg weakness, unsteadiness, seizures, and eventually paralysis or death. Beriberi, a disease marked by inflammatory or degenerative changes in the nerves, digestive systerm, and heart, can also result from B1 deficiencies. Birds with a vitamin B1 deficiency will have an unhealthy look and lack vigor. Avoid foods that have certain preservatives added (sulphides and nitrates) because these chemicals will break down B1. Appetite will also be decreased.

Symptoms of Toxicity: Not reported in birds.

Found: B1 is found in whole grains, such as cereal grains, peanuts, peas, raisins, oranges, dried beans, lentils, red kidney beans, sesame seeds, Brazil nuts, almonds, pecans, asparagus, potatoes, and brewer's yeast.

Riboflavin (B2)

Function: Riboflavin, also known as B2, is involved in the release of energy from proteins, carbohydrates, and fats in food. Also important for reproduction.

Symptoms of a Deficiency: A deficiency in B2 results in slow growth, low egg production, diarrhea, and leg paralysis in growing birds. Disorders associated with the nervous system, gastrointestinal system, and skeleton are usually observed. Fatty liver has also been detected.

Symptoms of Toxicity: Causes the urine to become a bright yellow color, which should not be confused with liver disease. Toxicity of B2 is rare because it is excreted in the urine.

Found: Riboflavin is found in eggs, milk, yogurt, beef liver, brewer's yeast, almonds, cottage cheese, cheddar cheese, yogurt, chicken, asparagus, broccoli, brussels sprouts, spinach, and whole-wheat bread.

Niacin

Function: Niacin is involved in many different body processes. It aids in the breakdown of fats and proteins and in red blood cell formation. Also important in reproduction.

Symptoms of a Deficiency: A deficiency of niacin can cause pellagra. Signs of pellagra are inflammation of the tongue and mouth, as well as poor feathering and a scaly dermatitis of the feet and the head. Nervousness can also be observed.

Symptoms of Toxicity: While in people it can cause both the cholesterol and triglycerine levels to decrease, it can also cause the blood vessels to dilate. This may result in indigestion, itchy skin, liver damage, ulcers, and an increase in glucose. These problems are not always seen in birds.

Found: Niacin is found in all foods, but the highest amounts are in animal products. In plants, it is poorly absorbed. Rice polishings, as well as yeast, are rich sources of niacin. You can also find niacin in chicken, beef, peanut butter, tuna, peanuts, sesame seeds, sunflower seeds, brewer's yeast, salmon, eggs, peas, and potatoes.

Biotin (B7)

Function: Biotin is necessary for many different body functions, including those that manufacture and break down fats, amino acids, and carbohydrates. Biotin is stored in the liver. A biotin or B7 deficiency is unlikely unless the bird is on a diet that consists mainly of wheat or barley with no other supplements.

Symptoms of a Deficiency: If the bird develops a B7 deficiency, the signs are usually fatty liver and kidney syndrome. Dermatitis of the feet may develop, with calluses and hemorrhagic cracks indicating signs of infection. Lesions may also appear around the eyes as well as the beak.

Symptoms of Toxicity: Not reported in pet birds.

Found: Products that are excellent sources of biotin are liver, tuna, oatmeal, soybeans, eggs, peanut butter, brown or white rice, chicken, bananas, and brewer's yeast.

Folic Acid

Function: Folic acid functions in the formation of uric acid and is very important in the excretion of wastes through the kidneys. This makes folic acid crucial to the avian diet.

Symptoms of a Deficiency: Signs of a folic acid deficiency are slow growth, poor feathering, failure of the feather to pigment normally, and anemia, with abnormally formed red blood cells. The immune system can also be affected. Long-term antibiotic use can also cause a deficiency.

Symptoms of Toxicity: Signs are anemia and fattiness of the heart, liver, and kidney.

Found: Yeast, alfalfa, spinach, broccoli, some cereals, chick peas, oranges, peanuts, brussels sprouts, wheat germ, red beans, bananas, whole wheat bread, and wheat bran are rich sources of folic acid. Folic acid is also produced by bacteria in the bowels.

Cobalamine (B12)

Function: B12 (Cyanocobalamine or cobalamine) is necessary for maximum growth in young birds. It is also important in reproduction.

Symptoms of a Deficiency: B12 is a vitamin in which signs of deficiency are slow to appear. If a B12 deficiency is present, signs will be anemia, gizzard erosion, bending of the hock and a slipping of the tendon off the joint, and fattiness of the heart, liver, and kidney.

Symptoms of Toxicity: Not reported in pet birds.

Found: Even though bacteria in the gut can produce B12, it is not a dependable source. Vitamin supplements provide adequate supplies of B12. Feeding cooked liver is another way. It is also found in eggs, lean meat, brewer's yeast, wheat germ, soybeans, peanuts, and peas.

Pantothenic Acid (B3)

Function: Pantothenic acid is involved with the production of fats, cholesterol, bile, vitamin D, red blood cells, and some hormones and neurotransmitters.

Symptoms of a Deficiency: A B3 deficiency usually results in slow growth and ragged feathering. A dermatitis affecting the eyes, mouth, and the vent can occur.

Symptoms of Toxicity: Though not reported in pet birds, in humans it can cause diarrhea.

Found: Seed diets are adequate in supplying pantothenic acid. It can be found also in eggs, chicken, soybeans, peanut butter, bananas, potatoes, broccoli, beef liver, grapefruit, corn, cauliflower, eggs, rice, cantaloupe, wheat germ, and bread.

Pyridoxine (B6)

Function: Pyridoxine functions in the building and breaking down of carbohydrates, fats, and proteins, but it is mainly involved with proteins and amino acids.

Symptoms of a Deficiency: A deficiency results in poor growth, loss of appetite, weakness in the skeletal system, convulsions, poor egg production, and nervous disorders.

Symptoms of Toxicity: In some animals, it can cause stones in the kidneys or the bladder. However, it has not been reported in psittacines.

Found: B6 is found in both plants and animal products, and very little is stored in the body. Most practical diets require the addition of B6 for growth. Bananas, corn, sunflower seeds, brussels sprouts, some cereals, squash, chicken, potatoes, grapefruit, spinach, rice, peas, walnuts, and peanut butter are good sources.

Ascorbic acid (vitamin C) aids in the healing of wounds and forms a protective barrier against infection. Vitamin C can be found in citrus fruits, broccoli, carrots, and many other fruits and vegetables.

Ascorbic Acid (Vitamin C)

Function: Ascorbic acid aids in the formation and maintenance of a protein that forms the basis in connective tissue, as well as the supporting material in the blood vessel wall, and it helps to bind the muscle tissue together. It aids in the healing of wounds, fractures, bruises, and forms a protective barrier against infections or disease. Some birds need vitamin C added to their diet, while other birds can manufacture enough in their livers or kidneys. Vitamin C is safe to add to diets because, as a water-soluble vitamin, any excess flushes out of the bird's system rather than being stored in the body like many supplements.

Symptoms of a Deficiency: A lack of vitamin C could cause a decreased resistance to infection, as well as a loss of body tissue integrity.

Symptoms of Toxicity: While this water-soluble vitamin is normally excreted by the kidneys, in some animals, kidney stones have formed.

Found: Citrus fruits, strawberries, pears, a variety of buds, shoots, and tropical fruit, such as kiwi, papaya, and mangos are all excellent sources of vitamin C. It is also found in brussels sprouts, broccoli, green peppers, tomatoes, cantaloupe, cabbage, asparagus, green peas, potatoes, lima beans, bananas, and carrots.

Choline

Function: Choline is important in controlling fat and cholesterol in the body; it helps in preventing fat from accumulating around the liver. It also helps to regulate the kidneys and liver. It is also important for proper nerve transmission.

Symptoms of a Deficiency: A deficiency of choline can result in fatty liver disease, heart problems, kidney problems, and bony deposits.

Symptoms of Toxicity: Not reported

Found: Cabbage, egg yolks, liver, nuts, lentils, and cauliflower.

Minerals

Minerals make up about five percent of body weight. In body fluids, minerals occur mainly as salts. When placed in a solution, these salts break down into their component ions. These ions, or electrolytes, are charged particles, either positively charged (cations), or negatively charged (anions). They act together to maintain the osmotic pressure in all the body fluids.

Minerals are, as the term suggests, essential to the overall health, both physical and mental, of an organism. The other minerals, also vital but needed in smaller amounts, are the trace minerals.

Calcium

Function: Calcium is important because of its involvement in the development of bones and muscles, blood coagulation, and nerve impulse transmission. Calcium is important in egg production, as most people would guess, because eggshell is 85 percent calcium. Calcium works together with magnesium to aid in the normal contractions of muscles, including the most important muscle, the heart. Vitamin D3, calcium, and phosphorus are all connected. Poor calcium absortion is the result of high phosphorus levels, which lowers the vitamin D3 levels, and then calcium is not absorbed properly.

Symptoms of a Deficiency: A deficiency of calcium can cause rickets, bone and joint problems, a thinner eggshell, egg binding, and seizures.

Symptoms of Toxicity: In some birds, kidney failure has occured.

Found: Sources of calcium are dark-green leafy vegetables, broccoli, dried beans and peas, bone meal, cuttlebone, kale, turnip greens, yogurt, tofu, and cheeses.

Phosphorus

Function: Phosphorus is needed for growth, maintenance, and repair of all the body tissues, and the strong structure and functioning of bones. Phosphorus converts carbohydrates, proteins, and fats into energy and is a component of cell membranes. (See calcium.)

Symptoms of a Deficiency: Phosphorus deficiencies result in bone and joint problems, muscle weakness, and slow healing.

Symptoms of Toxicity: Can result in a calcium deficiency. This is because toxicity can upset the proper balance of the calcium/phosphorus ratio.

Found: Good sources of phosphorus are milk, cereal grains, fishmeal, liver, yogurt, chicken, peanut butter, almonds, lima beans, kidney beans, potatoes, eggs, broccoli, and whole wheat bread.

Potassium

Function: Potassium is necessary in regulating body fluids and in the transmission and function of the nervous system. Potassium also helps to maintain the contraction and relaxation of muscles and the metabolism of carbohydrates.

Symptoms of a Deficiency: Potassium deficiencies result in very slow growth, kidney disease, fragile bones, muscle weakness, paralysis, and seizures.

Symptoms of Toxicity: May cause heart failure.

Found: Good sources are bananas, apricots, potatoes, squash, peanuts, split peas, beef, oranges, cantaloupe, grains, fruits, and vegetables.

Sulfur

Function: Sulfur is a component of proteins, insulin, thiamin, and biotin. It is also involved with the storage as well as the release of energy. Sulfur is a part of the genetic material in cells.

Symptoms of a Deficiency: A deficiency of sulfur would result in problems associated with protein deficiencies and in fatty liver disease.

Symptoms of Toxicity: Can affect the proper absorption and excretion of copper and molybdenum. Other toxicities have not yet been studied in pet birds.

Found: Sulfur is present in protein diets and in chicken, eggs, meat, liver, dried beans and peas, and milk.

Sodium

Function: Sodium is found in fluids outside of the cells in the body. Absorption occurs mostly in the small intestines, though a small amount is absorbed in the stomach. The kidneys help to maintain normal blood levels of sodium. Sodium helps to neutralize acid-forming elements in the body. It is essential for glucose absorption and to transport nutrients across the cellular membranes. It also helps to maintain the volume of the body's fluid.

Symptoms of a Deficiency: A deficiency of sodium can cause internal disorders, poor growth and reproduction, and softening of bones. An excess can cause the cells to absorb too much water, causing swelling.

Symptoms of Toxicity: Excessive thirst and respiratory difficulties are the main problems.

Found: Good sources of sodium are eggs, kale, carrots, Swiss chard, celery, and spinach. As a whole, nuts are low in sodium, unless they contain added salt.

Sodium is necessary for proper glucose absorption and for transporting nutrients across cellular membranes, and it is found in eggs, carrots, and celery.

Chlorine

Function: Chlorine helps to maintain the distribution and normal balance of fluids throughout the system. This, in turn, helps to maintain the normal pH balance. Chlorine, being a component of stomach acid, aids in digestion.

Symptoms of a Deficiency: A deficiency upsets the body's fluid balance and produces poor digestion, muscle weakness, lethargy, and a failure to thrive.

Symptoms of Toxicity: Not known in pet birds.

Found: It can be found in meat, chicken, grains, some fruits and vegetables, nuts, and salt.

Magnesium

Function: Magnesium is involved in converting carbohydrates, proteins, and fats into energy, in the manufacture of proteins, and in the removal of toxic substances. It is important for muscle control. It helps with muscle relaxation and contraction and nerve transmission. Most avian diets have ingredients that are rich in magnesium, which makes a deficiency very unlikely. In young birds, a deficiency can cause convulsions or sometimes death.

Symptoms of a Deficiency: If an unlikely deficiency should happen, signs would include poor growth, lethargy, and when very severe, it can cause neuromuscular hyperirritability, which could result in death.

Symptoms of Toxicity: Poor egg production with thin shells have been reported, along with diarrhea.

Found: Peanuts, nuts, bananas, dried beans and peas, whole grains, peanut butter, dark leafy-green vegetables, chickpeas, figs, and breads are some sources.

Silicon

Function: Silicon is the second-most abundant element in nature, the first being oxygen. Silicon is necessary for proper growth and development.

Symptoms of a Deficiency: An interesting discovery is that levels of silicon in the tissues decrease with age.

Symptoms of Toxicity: Not reported.

Found: Sources of silicon are whole grains, breads and cereals, beans, peas, and other vegetables. This mineral borders on the line between being a trace mineral and a macro or bulk element.

Copper

Function: Copper is essential to life. Blood and bone depend on it for proper function.

Symptoms of a Deficiency: A deficiency can cause weakness in the blood vessels and can cause an enlargement of the heart. Anemia and bone deformities have also been seen. Most diet supplements have adequate levels of copper.

Symptoms of Toxicity: Liver, kidney, and gizzard damage have been reported.

Found: It can be found in dried beans, chicken, nuts, cereals, peas, and dark-green leafy vegetables.

Iodine

Function: Iodine is necessary for the formation of thyroid hormones. It can cause baldness in some birds. (Do not confuse this with the bald spot that some lutino cockatiels have; this is a genetic problem.)

Symptoms of a Deficiency: A deficiency results in an enlargement of the thyroid gland and a reduction of the production of the thyroid hormones, plus poor growth, poor egg production, and reduced egg size.

Symptoms of Toxicity: Enlarged thyroid glands have been reported.

Found: Products, such as sea salt, seafood, kelp, and iodized salt, are excellent sources of iodine.

Selenium

Function: Selenium works together with enzymes to repair damage by oxidizing chemicals in the body.

Symptoms of a Deficiency: A deficiency can interfere with the reproductive system.

Symptoms of Toxicity: Abnormal feather condition, poor hatchability, and shock have been reported.

Found: Most commercial diets have adequate levels of selenium. It can also be found in cereal grains, chicken, egg noodles, tuna, granola, and some vegetables.

Iron

Function: Iron is the oxygen-carrying component in the blood.

Symptoms of a Deficiency: An iron deficiency can result in red blood cell reduction and anemia.

Symptoms of Toxicity: Abdominal pain and either diarrhea or constipation have been reported. In severe cases, even death has resulted. Because the liver is where iron is stored, amounts of excessive iron damage the liver, which can sometimes result in death.

Found: Liver, nuts, dried fruits, dried beans and peas, raisins, whole grains, strawberries, broccoli, brussels sprouts, winter squash, blackberries, spinach, pumpkin seeds, sunflower seeds, soybeans, almonds, Swiss chard, lentils, chicken, potatoes, and bananas are some sources.

Manganese

Function: Manganese aids in the formation of connective tissues, fats and cholesterol, bones, blood clotting factors, and proteins.

Symptoms of a Deficiency: Out of all the minerals, manganese deficiencies are the most likely to be found in the avian diet. It causes the bones to shorten and thicken, which can cause the hock joint to acquire a bend, allowing the tendon to slip off its joint. Birds with a manganese deficiency will sometimes "star gaze," which is when their heads and beak point straight up in the air, giving them the appearance of staring into space.

Symptoms of Toxicity: Very rare.

Found: Most avian diets have manganese supplements added to make sure growing birds don't have a deficiency problem. Some sources are spinach, whole grain breads, cereals, raisins, blueberries, wheat bran, dried beans and peas, and nuts. Cuttlebones and eggshells are other good sources.

In order for your bird to thrive, like this lilac-crowned Amazon Parrot, make sure there is enough zinc in his diet— many avian diets are near a deficiency of this mineral.

Zinc

Function: Some of zinc's functions include the mineralization of bone, the digestion of protein, and conversion of calories to energy. Zinc also aids in the regulation of blood-sugar, the maintenance of the genetic code, wound healing, and the strength of the immune system.

Symptoms of a Deficiency: Unfortunately, many avian diets border on the brink of inadequate zinc. Things to watch for are slow and poor growth, ratty and frayed feathers, and a thickening of the hock joint.

Symptoms of Toxicity: While overdoses can interfere with the proper absorption of selenium, it can also cause problems with the gizzard and the pancreas, and it can cause anorexia.

Found: Some sources are poultry, beef, cheddar cheese, brown rice, noodles, soybeans, eggs, potatoes, peanut butter, whole-grain breads, cereals, lima beans, yogurt, nuts, and spinach.

Cobalt

Function: Cobalt, a component of vitamin B12, aids in the formation of normal red blood cells, in the maintenance of nerve tissue, and the normal formation of other cells.

Symptoms of a Deficiency: A cobalt deficiency is connected to a deficiency of B12. Weakness and anemia, as well as a loss of appetite, can result.

Symptoms of Toxicity: It has not been reported in pet birds.

Found: Cobalt is found in most foods, but liver and muscle meat are the highest source. Foods of plant origin also contain cobalt.

Molybdenum

Function: Found in the skin, muscles, bones, and liver, molybdenum is a component of xanthine oxidase, an enzyme that acts in the formation of uric acid, and is important in the mobilization of iron. It is also necessary for proper growth and development.

Symptoms of a Deficiency: There has been no syndrome that points to a molybdenum deficiency.

Symptoms of Toxicity: In some animals, symptoms similar to gout have been reported.

Found: Some sources of molybdenum are liver, wheat germ, whole grains, dried peas and beans, fruits and vegetables grown in molybdenum-rich soil, and dark-green leafy vegetables.

Chromium

Function: Chromium is part of the group of elements that is also known as micro minerals. Micro minerals, as of this writing, have not been as well researched or documented as the other vitamins and minerals. Chromium functions as a component of the glucose-tolerant factor, also known as GTF. GTF works with insulin to regulate the metabolism of glucose by increasing the action of insulin.

Symptoms of a Deficiency: A deficiency of chromium prevents insulin from its normal function. Chromium is suspected to play a role in the configuration of RNA.

Symptoms of Toxicity: Not reported in pet birds.

Found: Good sources of chromium are whole grains, meats, cheese, eggs, yeast, molasses, puffed rice, buckwheat, wheat germ, and orange juice.

Fluoride

Function: Fluoride is found throughout the body fluids and bones. Fluoride may also aid in wound healing, as well as enhancing iron absorption.

Symptoms of a Deficiency: Though deficiencies of fluoride are rarely found, when it does occur, the bird can become more prone to osteoporosis and other bone-degenerating conditions.

Symptoms of Toxicity: In some animals, poor growth, weight loss, poor appetite, and bone deformities have been reported.

Found: Fluoride that is added in different amounts from city to city has been known to cause intestinal upsets. If you are traveling with your bird, bring along your own water to prevent any temporary upset. The best source of flouride is city water.

Nickel

Function: Nickel is found throughout the body, but is seen in greater amounts in the pancreas. The need for nickel in Psittacines is unknown; however, research has shown that it is an essential trace mineral in chicks as well as other animals. It is believed to be necessary for normal skin, cell membranes, and the metabolism of DNA. For unknown reasons, the amount of nickel present in the body doubles after severe burning, heart attacks, or strokes. It is poorly absorbed and can be toxic at high levels. It is truly a trace mineral since so little is necessary.

Symptoms of a Deficiency: If a deficiency is present (though this is unlikely), the skin changes colors and eruptions are seen, the legs thicken, and swelling may occur in the hocks. Structural changes occur as well as changes in the liver.

Symptoms of Toxicity: Not reported in pet birds.

Found: Good sources of nickel are green, leafy vegetables, whole seeds, fruits, and nuts.

Trace Minerals and Elements

Other trace elements include: arsenic (believed to control harmful intestinal organisms), bromine (found to increase the growth rate of chicks), vanadium (might take part in promoting growth and in the lowering of cholesterol). Other trace elements, such as tin, rubidium, aluminum, titanium, gallium, lithium, cesium, lead, gold, silver, radium, germanium, antimony, bismuth, strontium, cadmium, boron, barium, uranium, zirconium, and niobium are being researched in humans as of this writing. Found in extremely minute amounts in the body, it is not yet known what function these have in humans, let alone what function these trace elements play in avian nutrition.

As usual, everything points to the importance of a varied diet for our birds.

Amino Acids

There are two types of amino acids: the essential amino acids and the non-essential. While most of the information gathered here was on humans, it can also be applied to birds. Unlike with human medicine, not much research has been done on amino acids and birds.

Essential amino acids must be consumed daily because the bird can not manufacture them in his own body. Essential amino acids include: arginine, histidine, isoleucine, leucine, lysine, methionine, phenylalanine, threonine, tryptophan, and valine. Non-essential amino acids include: alanine, aspartic acid, citrulline, cysteine, crystine, glutamic acid, glycine, hydroxyproline, serine, taurine, and tyrosine.

Non-essential Amino Acids

Serine

Serine helps to form cysteine and aids in the formation of lecithin, cephalin and sphingomyelin.

Taurine

Taurine helps to regulate the nervous system. It is also a sulfur-containing amino acid. Taurine requires methionine for its biosynthesis in the body. It is also believed to help with the muscular system and is needed for proper growth. Present in animal products, it is not found in plants.

Tyrosine

Tyrosine plays a role in the brain's neurotransmitters, such as dopamine and epinephrine. In humans, it has been used to treat PMS, stress, depression, and drug abuse. Lab animal studies have been conducted as to tyrosine's ability to lower stress levels. However, it has been found to raise blood pressure.

Glutamic Acid

Glutamic acid has been found (in humans) to help inhibit the affects of senility and to counter the affects of depression. It once claimed to be a brain drug, helping to increase the IQ of mentally challenged individuals, though this is now proving to be untrue.

Cystine

Cystine is important as the primary protein of keratin. There have been reports that it helps to increase the lifespan in humans as well as fight the affects of arthritis. This non-essential amino acid contains sulfur in a state that helps to protect the cells. It is found in eggs, meats, dairy products, and in some cereals.

Aspartic Acid

Aspartic acid is an non-essential amino acid. Studies are being conducted by several researchers, and it is believed to help fight fatigue. In humans, it has been found to give us more energy.

Glutamic Acid

Glutamic acid helps to form proline and hydroxyproline.

Glycine

Glycine helps to form serine and also aids the formation of purines and porphyrins.

Essential Amino Acids

Arginine

Arginine aids in feather formation, as well as helping in normal muscle development. It is also considered to play a role in growth and in healing. It has been found to have liver-protecting properties, as well as functioning as an anti-cancer agent. It also plays a role in keeping the immune system healthy.

In large doses, it can cause bone and skin problems, and it can also have affects on the metabolic system. It is found in raw cereals, cola drinks, peanuts, cashews, barley, and peas. One drawback to this amino acid is that it promotes the growth of the herpes virus.

Histidine

Histidine is found in the hemoglobin. It helps to form glutamic acid and histamine and has been found to help increase thc activity of T cells. It is now used in studies to treat patients suffering from rhcumatoid arthritis.

Lysine

Lysine is the precursor of the substance in collagen. While arginine may help to promote the growth of herpes, lysine, on the other hand, inhibits its growth and can suppress growth in immature chicks.

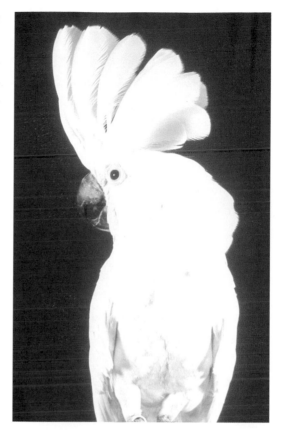

Arginine is an essential amino acid that aids in healthy feather formation, such as that displayed in the crest of this umbrella cockatoo.

It is found in milk and other dairy products, in potatoes, and in brewer's yeast. Lysine, along with methionine, is the amino acid that is most likely to be missing in the diet of pet birds.

Methionine

Methionine is necessary for normal muscle development, as well as the synthesis of choline. This is another sulfur-containing amino acid. It helps to remove fatty substances which may clog the arteries. Found in eggs, milk, liver, and fish, methionine, along with lysine, is an amino acid most likely to be missing in the diet of pet birds.

Phenylalanine

Phenylalanine is found in three forms. As D-Phenylalanine, it helps to alleviate chronic pain. As L-Phenylalanine, studies have suggested that it increases mental alertness and controls substance abuse symptoms. It can also control the appetite. However, it can also increase blood pressure. DL-Phenylalanine has been used to treat the pain associated with arthritis and fibrositis.

Threonine

Threonine helps prevent fat from storing up in the liver, aids in digestion and intestinal tract functions, and also aids in metabolism.

Tryptophan

Tryptophan is the precursor of serotonin and niacin. It has been used (in humans) to treat jet lag, as a sleeping aid, as an appetite suppressant, as treatment for substance abuse, as a pain reliever, and to inhibit panic attacks. On the downside, it has been found to cause bladder cancer, severe liver disorders, and is considered to be toxic in high doses.

Valine

Valine is one of three essential amino acids that are considered to be in the branch-chain group. When working together they have been used to help prevent the neurological problems that occur in chronic liver disease. The three together also help to restore muscle mass. In humans, these amino acids have been used in a study with patients with Lou Gehrig disease (ALS). So far, these studies are proving useful. Valine is part of pantothenic acid and is the precursor of leucine.

Protein

Protein is another necessary requirement for a bird's diet. Protein is the substance that the body uses to build tissues, muscles, skin, beaks, nails, feathers, body organs, eggs, and even the blood (hemoglobin). Growing feathers need a continuous source of protein and other nutrients to maintain their healthy appearance.

Protein is either of plant or animal origin and is a good source of amino acids. While some sources may be high in one amino acid, they may be lacking in others. This is why variety is so important.

Protein in avian diets that have all the amino acids are called complete proteins.

Complete proteins are all of animal origin, which is why eggs are so healthy for our birds. Protein deficiencies can result in feather plucking, weight loss, egg eating, poor feathering, and deaths of newly hatched babies. Birds can also develop protein toxicities, where they may show signs of poisoning, such as sleeplessness, troubled breathing, severe diarrhea, and even death.

A study using baby cockatiels was made to determine the amount of protein that was needed for optimal development. It was found that 20 percent crude protein was needed for optimal development, while 10 to 15 percent protein resulted in stunted development and even some deaths. Even worse, 5 percent protein was found to produce babies with severe

Protein is necessary for building your bird's tissues, muscles, skin, beak, nails, and feathers.

stunted development, which resulted in 100 percent mortality rate, and 25 percent protein was found to cause behavioral problems, including aggression. Using 35 percent protein in the diet resulted in severe depressed growth and aggression.

Carbohydrates

Carbohydrates are the main source of energy and heat, and most are plant products. Carbohydrates are either sugars or starches. Extra carbohydrates are changed into fat and stored in the tissues. Birds do not usually suffer from a deficiency of carbohydrates. While there is no specific requirements for the amount of carbohydrates in a bird's diet, it should balance the protein intake. Good sources of carbohydrates for birds are wheat, oats, rice, and canary seed.

Fats

Small amounts of fat are needed in pet bird diets. They also provide energy and heat. Besides this, they act as carriers for fat soluble vitamins, fatty acids, and minerals. Fat is needed in a bird's diet to keep the skin soft and the feathers in good condition.

Fats contain fatty acids, but only three are essential. The essential fatty acids are linoleic, linolenic, and arachidonic. Birds need linoleic acid for growth and reproduction. A deficiency will result in decreased fertility and smaller eggs. Dietary fat also helps in the absorption and the utilization of the fat-soluble vitamins (A, D, E, and K). It also aids in the absorption of beta-carotenes from non-fat sources that can be converted to vitamin A.

Found in safflower seeds, sunflower seeds, and flax, fats should be fed only in limited amounts because too much can lead to obesity. As the high fat content in the diet increases, so does the cholesterol level. High cholesterol levels can lead to blocked arteries and to heart disease. High fat diets are one of the causes (but not the only cause) of fatty liver disease.

Special Diets and Nutritional Needs

Different Species, Different Needs

Not all birds are created equal. Birds come from different regions of the world, and the food that they eat in the wild has different nutritional values from region to region. Therefore, it stands to reason that captive-born birds will also have different nutritional needs.

Though some studies on avian nutrition were conducted back in the 1980s and a few seed and pellet manufacturers have done studies, not much has really been published. Therefore, before putting your bird on any specific diet, check with your avian veterinarian first. The following information can serve as a general guide, however, for the different nutritional needs of different species of birds.

Amazons

Amazons may have a tendency to have vitamin-A deficiencies. Amazons need to have a diet that includes squash, pumpkin, spinach, red chili peppers, and other foods rich in vitamin A. Amazons also have a tendency to be overweight, so they also need a diet that limits foods that are lower in fat. Amazons should also be a fed a diet that is lower in protein.

Avian nutrition is still in its infancy. With more than 350 different species of parrots, many of whom are either threatened or endangered, we may never really know what each individual species needs. However, like people, a healthy, varied diet is the key to good health. If you feed a wide variety of healthy foods, your bird will be receiving all the vitamins and minerals he needs to keep him healthy.

Remember: As always, see your avian veterinarian at least once a year.

Eclectus parrots, like this male and female, may have a higher need for vitamin A in their diets than most birds.

Eclectus

Eclectus may have a higher need for vitamin A in their diets.

African Greys, Cockatoos, and Cockatiels

Greys, cockatoos, cockatiels, and your powder birds may need diets that are rich in calcium. Excellent sources of calcium are found in dark-green leafy vegetables, dried beans and peas, kale, turnip greens, bone meal, tofu, and in dairy products. However, dairy products should be used sparingly because birds are lactose intolerant.

Macaws

Macaws may require a diet that is higher in fat. They also need a diet that consists of a wide variety of nuts, and some species need a diet that is lower in protein.

Hyacinth macaws are specialized eaters in the wild. They eat mainly the nuts from the Scheelea palm and the Atalea palm. They need to be feed macadamia nuts, Brazil nuts, walnuts, coconuts, pecans, and other nuts. They require more fat and carbohydrates and less protein in their diets. Remember that hyacinths are very big birds and they eat a lot. They are also very slow to wean.

This Congo African Grey—and Cockatoos, Cockatiels, and other African Greys, may require diets that are rich in calcium. Dark-green, leafy vegetables and dried beans and peas are good sources.

Conures should be given a diet that is rich in Vitamin K, high in fat, and lower in protein.

Conures

Conures require a diet that is higher in fat and lower in protein. Conures should also be given vegetables that are rich in vitamin K. (Conures are prone to Conure Bleeding Syndrone, which could be caused by a lack of vitamin K.)

Lories and Lorikeets

Lories and lorikeets need a diet that is higher in carbohydrates and lower in protein. Their diet should contain no more than 15 percent protein. The primary diet of lories and lorikeets is fruit and nectar. They should not be given seeds because their gizzards are weaker than other birds and cannot grind up the seeds. Lots of fruits and fresh greens should be given as a supplement to their diet.

Special Diets for Weaning Baby Birds

Why is it so important that baby birds receive a varied diet from early on? Like human children, proper nutrition plays an important role in both the health and development of the rapidly growing avian bodies. Bones are developing, feathers are growing, and eating habits are developing. A bird that learns to eat properly when young will develop healthy eating habits later on.

Weaning is a stressful time. Weaning is a time of adjustment for birds–they are learning to adjust to their envirnoment, and they are also learning to eat on their own. Stress is hard on the body, but a body that is receiving proper nutrition is better at fighting off any illness.

Weaning should never be forced. Forced weaning can cause behavior problems as the bird matures. Just because a certain species of bird should be weaned after four months does not mean that that particular bird is ready to be weaned. Weaning should be a slow, easy process.

Necessary Veterinary Checkups

Veterinary evaluations are just as important to your bird's health as good nutrition is. Veterinary checkups can also indicate how healthy your bird's diet really is and if he needs vitamins, supplements, or any changes in his diet. Therefore, take your bird to his veterinarian once a year for a full physical and blood panel.

The following are just a few of the benefits of giving your bird a veterinary checkup at least once a year:

- The veterinarian can see what is normal for the bird, so if your bird does get sick, he or she will know what is not normal.
- Blood work can show disease or problems even before symptoms develop.
- The veterinarian will be able to tell you if you need to change anything in the bird's daily habits, such as diet, adding supplements or vitamins, exercise, etc.
- The veterinarian can answer any questions you have about your bird and his care.

Abundance Weaning

Weaning is a great time to start introducing new foods. Baby birds are very curious and they taste their environment. They are very open to trying everything. The best way to wean a baby is through abundance weaning.

Abundance weaning is a relatively new concept where a wide variety and quantity of weaning foods are available all day long. Foods that can go bad quickly are replaced hourly. In addition to this, foods are also offered from the fingers to the baby. Various seed and pellet manufacturers have developed special weaning foods that can be fed right from your fingers. Feeding foods directly from your fingers is similar to the parent birds feeding the babies themselves. I have found that it meets many of the physiological needs of the baby. It also helps with the bonding process. All of my birds that were weaned in this way are very healthy and happy and not one of my birds who is older than 20 years has any behavior problems. Even the babies that went to different homes are all doing great.

How to Feed Weaning Babies

Food needs to be cut up into small pieces. Offer a wide range of foods. Babies are curious and will be attracted to different colors, shapes, textures, and even different presentations. While I was weaning all of my birds, I offered almost every variety of fruit and vegetables my grocery store had to offer. This was in addition to the pastas, the beans, legumes, rices, cereals, meats, and other foods. My family was drooling with envy at all the varieties of food that the babies were eating. While my human kids turn their noses

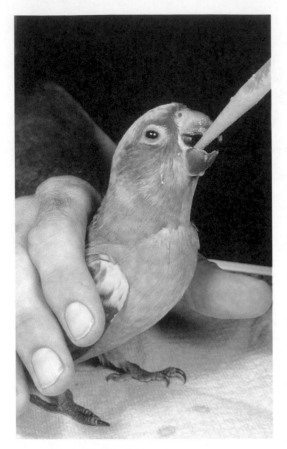

It is a good idea to offer food to your bird with a syringe even after he is weaned; this way it will be easier to feed him medication should he ever need it.

up at anything new, all my birds dive in with enthusiasm at anything put into their dishes.

Another tip on weaning is to offer foods warm, not hot. Hot foods can cause crop burn, which could seriously injure or kill the bird.

Another thing to keep in mind is to offer food in a variety of different dishes. One lady I knew offered her bird foods in a blue-colored crock. The crock eventually broke, and when she used a different-colored crock, the bird would not eat. He wanted his blue-colored dish. Therefore, by offering different colors and sizes, you can prevent this from happening.

Even after the baby is weaned, it is still a good idea to continue offering food with either the syringe or by spoon. If you ever have to medicate the bird, it will be easier on him and you if he will take the medicine from the spoon or syringe.

Weaning Foods

The following is a list of general foods that will provide the appropriate amount of nutrients for weaning birds when fed in variety and in a balanced diet.

Grains, Breads, and Muffins

Corn bread

Graham crackers

Mandel bread, soaked

Matzoh

Matzoh balls

Mini bagels

Oatmeal

Pastas

Rice

Rice cakes

Rice Chex

Rice Krispies

Sweetened corn cereals

Sweetened oat cereals

Toasted bread

Unsalted crackers

Unsalted, unbuttered popcorn

Wheat cereals

Whole-wheat or multigrained bread

Zweibach toast, soaked

Other grains

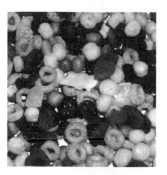

Vegetables

When served as weaning foods, the following vegetables should be cut into small pieces and cooked.

Beans

Beets

Broccoli

Carrots

Corn

Green beans

Jalapeno peppers

Lima beans

Mixed vegetables

Okra

Peas

Potatoes

Summer squash

Sweet potatoes

Winter squash

Yams

Fruit

Before serving these fruits to your baby birds, they need to be cut into small pieces.

Apple

Bananas

Berries (all kinds)

Grapes

Kiwis

Mangos

Melons

Oranges

Papaya

Pears

Star fruit

Winter squash

Yams

Other Foods

Hulled seeds

Millet spray

Monkey biscuits

Peanut butter sandwiches rolled in millet

Pellets

Scrambled eggs

Hard-boiled eggs

Sprouted seeds

Foods to Avoid and Other Hazards

While most foods that we eat are good for our birds, there are some that can be very harmful to them. The foods discussed in this chapter should *never* be fed to your birds.

Chocolate

Chocolate is a favorite among humans. However, to our feathered friends, it can be deadly. Chocolate contains theobromine, and even in small amounts it can kill a bird. The problem with chocolate is that it may not kill the bird right away, but the toxin will build up in the liver over time. When it reaches a toxic amount, the bird will start displaying neurological symptoms that will lead to death. These symptoms include depression, vomiting, convulsions, seizures, and eventually death. Other animals also should not be given chocolate.

Avocados

While it is the pit of the avocado that is poisonous, the flesh can become tainted with the toxin. There has been documentation of avocados killing small birds such as budgies and cockatiels.

Sugar

Too much sugar in a bird's diet has been reported to cause severe problems in the digestive system. Like with people, diets that are

Too much sugar can be dangerous, so always stick to natural sugars when feeding your bird, found in fruits and sweet vegetables, like corn.

high in sugar can precede diabetes. This has been reported in many cases when the bird's diet consisted of high-sugar treats and not enough healthy foods.

Because refined sugar has been heavily processed, there is little nutrient value left. Too much refined sugar can not only lead to diabetes, but it can also contribute to yeast infections, heart disorders, high cholesterol, and calcium imbalance. Too much sugar has also been linked to feather plucking, irritability, anxiety, and nervous disorders.

The best kind of sugar comes as natural sugars, which are found in fruits and in sweet vegetables like corn.

Old Seeds

It is always best to feed fresh seed and not any that has been kept around for a while. Old seed can contain fungus, mycotoxins and alfatoxins, which are lethal. When buying seed in quantity, freeze it and remove only a week's supply at a time. This will cut down on seed moths as well. Bad seed can cause weight loss, depression, and this can lead to death.

Never allow your birds near the stove when you are cooking. Many birds have fallen into boiling liquid or drowned in a pot of water while their owners were cooking. Keep your birds safe from this hazard—keep them out of the kitchen.

Mayonnaise Products

When a bird eats, the food is not immediately digested and may sit in the crop for a while. Mayonaise can go bad rather quickly, so it should be avoided.

Unwashed Fruits or Vegetables

Always wash any fruit or vegetables thoroughly before offering it to your bird. Many different pesticides could have been used before the fruit or vegetable got to market. Also, all kinds of bacteria could be on the skins. Even

Thoroughly wash any fruits or vegetables that you feed to your bird in order to remove pesticides and bacteria.

bananas should be washed. The peels may be contaminated with monkey urine. When peeled, some of this can get on your hands and can contaminate the inside.

Rhubarb

The leaves of this plant contain a chemical called oxalic acid which can become toxic to birds. Rhubarb contains high levels of oxalic acid. Oxalic acid can block calcium absorption. Some experts believe that the entire plant contains harmful levels of oxalic acid, while other experts believe that the stalks are safe because there are very low levels of it in the stalks. Rhubarb is not the only vegetable that contains oxalic acid. Spinach also contains it. While spinach is considered to be healthy for your bird, it is best to feed in small amounts.

Fruit Pits

Many of us enjoy eating fruits, but did you know that the pits of many fruits are deadly to your bird? And it's not just the pit that can be toxic. When you cut into a pitted fruit you may see a darker color in the flesh close to the pit—this is the toxin

from the pit that has bled into the fruit. If you want to give your bird fruit that has a pit, make sure that you cut out any discoloration around the pit. The pits and any discolored area around the pits are toxic, but the fruit itself is not. (The pits contain cyanide.) However, branches and leaves from a pitted fruit are also toxic to your bird.

Nuts

Even nuts such as Brazil nuts and almonds can cause problems for your bird. This is especially true around the holiday season when imported nuts are polished and also dyed. Most birds do not ingest the nut shells, but some birds may. The dyes in these nuts are hard to digest,

When buying nuts for your bird, only purchase nuts that have no dyes—the dyes are difficult for birds to digest.

so when birds eat these nuts, they may end up with impacted crops, which can lead to death. When buying nuts for your bird, buy from sources you can trust. Even imported nuts are safe as long as no dye has been added to them.

Dairy Products

Birds are lactose intolerant and therefore cannot metabolize dairy products. Feed occasionally and only in small amounts. Birds seem to tolerate dairy in baked products and when used in cooking.

As far as eggs are concerned, make sure that you always wash all shells before using. Eggs can also be a source of salmonella.

Mold

Mold is usually thought of as being present on peanuts. Mold is also present on other nuts, legumes, grains, fruits, and even vegetables. This is why it is important to use human-grade foods. Peanuts are usually talked about as being a source of molds. Alfatoxin can cause cancer, and it can be deadly if consumed in large enough amounts.

The Dangers of Nonstick Cookware and Appliances

Never cook using nonstick cookware if your bird lives in the house. Heated, nonstick cookware has a special coating, and this coating emits a colorless, odorless fume when heated that kills birds almost immediately. It was originally thought that only burned or overheated nonstick cookware emitted these dangerous fumes, but it was recently discovered that this cookware could kill birds even at normal cooking temperatures.

Nonstick coating can be found on griddles, pans, deep fryers, bread makers, crock pots, and many other kitchen utensils and appliances. To be safe, only use cookware made of stainless steel, copper, or other materials that do not have nonstick coating present.

The nonstick coating is not limited to cookware, either. Household items such as irons, portable heaters, heat lamps, hair dryers, curling irons, and ironing board covers can all emit these toxic fumes. Make sure your bird will not be anywhere near these potentially harmful fumes.

Caffeine

Caffeine is present in coffee and in sodas, and while not particularly healthy for humans, it can cause serious problems in birds. It can cause nervousness, hyperactivity, and irritability.

Salt

Highly salted foods are not healthy for anyone, but salt is especially not good for birds. Parrots do not excrete salt as humans do. As in humans, high blood pressure is one of the many bad side effects.

Alcohol

Never, never give your bird alcohol of any kind. A birds liver can't metabolize alcohol, even in small amounts. Also, it is cruel to give your bird alcohol just to watch him acting drunk.

Food Dyes

Many foods today have dyes added to them to make them more appealing to the eye. This is also true in bird foods.

Many food colorings are synthetic and are not natural. Synthetic food colors are sometimes derived from petroleum or coal tars. In high doses, these food dyes have caused cancer in lab rats. They are also linked to allergies and even behavioral disorders. According to the FDA, different dyes can cause different problems.

Red dye #3 has been linked to thyroid tumors, chromosomal damage, and hyperactivity. Red dye #40 has been linked to lymphatic tumors and hyperactivity. Blue dye #1 has been known to cause chromosomal damage, while blue dye # 2 has been linked to brain tumors. Green dye #3 can cause bladder tumors. Yellow dye #5 has been known to cause thyroid and lymphatic tumors, allergic reactions, and hyperactivity, and yellow dye #6 has caused kidney tumors, chromosomal damage, and allergic reactions.

It is best to use natural dyes in your bird's food (and in your diet as well).

Sulfites

Many dried fruits and vegetables contain sulfites to preserve them. Longer shelf life is what many consumers want. It also makes the fruit look better. However, like some humans, birds can react to these sulfites. Some birds may display bizarre behavior, including plucking and even aggression. Use dried fruits and vegetables from a health food store. These do not include sulfites in their foods.

Food Allergies

Like people, birds can develop allergies to foods. A recent food allergy that has been brought to my attention is spirulina. In cockatoos there have been many reports of aggression. When the spirulina was removed, the aggression also stopped.

There have also been reports of allergies to peanuts. Symptoms included plucking and aggression, as well as hyperactivity.

Part Two:

The Recipes

Breads and Muffins

Contents

Good Stuff Bread

³/₄ cup soy flour
1 cup whole wheat flour
1 cup all purpose flour
¹/₂ cup wheat germ
¹/₄ cup multi-grain flour
¹/₃ cup instant dry milk
2 tsp. baking powder
2 tsp. baking soda
1 pinch of salt

¹/₂ cup chopped nuts
¹/₂ cup chopped dates, dried
   cranberries, or raisins
1 cup plain yogurt or applesauce
1 egg, beaten with shells (washed)
¹/₄ cup oil
¹/₄ cup molasses
¹/₄ cup honey
¹/₂ cup orange juice or apple juice

Preheat the oven to 350°F.

Mix all of the dry ingredients in a large bowl. In a smaller bowl, mix together juice, honey, molasses, oil, egg, and yogurt (applesauce). Stir in dates, cranberries or raisins, and the nuts. Mix well and then stir into the dry ingredients until blended. Spoon into a greased, floured loaf pan, (9x5x3) and bake for 45-60 minutes or until it tests done with a toothpick.

I make this into small muffins instead of the bread. When making muffins, bake for 20-30 minutes or until done. My birds love it either way.

SAFETY TIP: When using egg shells, always make sure you wash them thoroughly first.

Leftovers Bread

1 box cornbread mix
2 eggs with shells (washed)

Anything else left over in the way of fruits, vegetables, beans, rice, etc.

Preheat oven to 350°F.

Follow the instructions on the cornbread mix. Mix everything together, blending well. Bake on a cookie sheet for 20-30 minutes or until a toothpick comes out clean. Cut into cubes and freeze. Feed one cube a day. Depending on the leftovers, you will need to adjust the liquid to make a batter of cornbread consistency.

This is great for leftovers that you didn't know what to do with. You can even use spaghetti and meatballs in this one.

Cornbread Squares

2 cups yellow cornmeal
1 tsp. baking powder
1 egg with shell (washed)
$1/2$ cup chunky apple sauce
$1/2$ cup natural apple juice

$1/3$ cup mixed vegetables
$1/3$ cup grated carrots
$1/3$ cup brown rice, cooked
$1/3$ cup mixed nuts

Preheat oven to 350°F.

Mix all the ingredients together, adding more juice if needed. Put in a greased 8x8 pan and bake for 35-45 minutes or until a toothpick comes out clean. Cool and cut into birdie-size squares. Place any leftovers into a plastic zip bag and freeze.

Blueberry Muffins

2 cups whole wheat flour
$1/2$ cup sugar
1 egg with shell (washed)
1 cup blueberries (fresh, if possible)
$1/2$ tsp. salt
$1/2$ tsp. nutmeg

3 tbs. margarine, melted
$1/2$ to 1 cup milk
$1/4$ cup millet
1 tbs. baking powder
1 tbs. spirulina (optional)
1 tbs. vitamins (optional)

TIP: You may find it easier to grind pellets up in a coffee bean grinder. If you use a food processor, you may have to make recipes in small batches.

Preheat oven to 350°F.

Grease muffin tins using non-stick spray or line with paper muffin sheets. Combine the dry ingredients. Add milk, egg, and margarine. Stir in blueberries. If mixture is too dry, add more milk tablespoon by tablespoon.

Bake around 30-35 minutes, or until a toothpick comes out clean.

When blueberries are in season, I make this for my birds. Other times I use a blueberry muffin mix.

Mega Bread

1 cup Kaytee pellets
1 cup millet
1 cup cornmeal
4 tbs. baking powder
$1/3$ cup wheat germ oil
$1/3$ cup vegetable oil
1 banana—very ripe, mashed
6 large eggs with shells (washed)

1 cup frozen mixed vegetables, thawed
1 cup cooked brown rice
1 cup cooked 15-bean mix
1 cup canned pumpkin (16 oz.)
2-4 tbs. applesauce
1 tsp. scraped cuttlebone or mineral block
Apple juice (only if mix is too dry)

Preheat oven to 350°F.

In a food processor, grind up the pellets. Add the remaining dry ingredients and process until mixed. Add the oils, mashed banana, and eggs with shells and process for around 1-2 minutes. Add the pumpkin and applesauce and process for around 1-2 more minutes.

Pour this mixture into a large bowl. Add the vegetables, rice, and the bean mix and stir until they are mixed in. If it is too dry, add some apple juice. If it is too wet, add more cornmeal. When the mixture is the consistency of corn bread, pour into a greased 9x13 baking pan. Bake around 35-45 minutes or until toothpick comes clean.

Rolled Treats

1 cup Kaytee pellets, finely ground
$1/2$ cup cornmeal
$1/2$ cup whole wheat flour
1 cup ground almonds
2 tbs. powdered wheat grass

1 cuttlebone, finely ground
4 eggs with shells (washed)
2 whole carrots, cooked and pureed
Apple juice, unsweetened, as needed

Preheat oven to 375°F.

Mix all the ingredients together, adding just enough juice to make it into a firm dough. If it's too moist, add more cornmeal or whole wheat flour. Scoop by spoonful and roll into small balls.

Place on a greased cookie sheet. Bake for 20-30 minutes. Cool. Makes around 90-100 balls. Freeze leftovers. For an added treat, roll in chopped nuts before cooking.

Sweet-and-Sour Muffins

2 cups whole wheat flour
$1/4$ cup wheat germ
$1/2$ cup sugar
2 eggs
$1/2$ cup unsweetened crushed
    pineapple

$1/2$ cup shredded carrots
$1/2$ cup chopped green peppers
$1/4$ cup apple juice
$3/4$ cup pineapple juice
1 tbs. baking powder
$1/2$ tsp. salt

HELPFUL HINT: If your bird won't eat spirulina, calcium, vitamins, or wheat grass sprinkled on top of his food, you can add these ingredients to almost every recipe. You can also finely grind up a cuttlebone or mineral block in the food processor and add to the above ingredients.

Preheat oven to 400°F.

Combine the dry ingredients. Add the apple juice, eggs, pineapple juice, carrots, crushed pineapple, and green peppers. Mix thoroughly. If too dry, add a little water. Pour into muffin tins sprayed with non-stick spray, or lined. Bake for 30-35 minutes or until toothpick comes out clean.

A very different-tasting muffin, but birds enjoy it.

Sweet Potato (Yams) Muffins

2 large sweet potatoes or yams,
    mashed
2 cups whole wheat flour
$1/4$ cup wheat germ
2 eggs with shells
1 tsp. salt

1 tsp. cinnamon
$1/4$ cup brown sugar
$1/2$ cup apple juice
$1/2$ cup chopped pecans
1 tbs. baking powder

Preheat the oven to 350°F.

Combine all the dry ingredients. Boil yams (or sweet potatoes) until tender. Save the water. Add eggs, juice, and mashed yams (sweet potatoes) to the dry ingredients. Stir in the pecans. If needed, add the water from the boiled yams. Prepare muffin tins using a nonstick spray, or line with cupcake liners. Bake around 30-35 minutes or until toothpick comes out clean. A great-tasting treat for Thanksgiving, these are so good you will be begging your bird for some.

SUBSTITUTION TIP: Instead of water, use carrot juice, papaya juice, etc. Check out the health food section.

A great recipe for people, too!

Tiny's Yummy Bread

This is one of Tiny's favorite treats. He loves all kinds of breads, but this one wins hand down.

3 1/2 cups flour
2/3 cup vegetable oil
1/2 cup sugar
1/2 cup brown sugar
4 large eggs with shells
1 cup canned pumpkin
1 cup applesauce
1/3 cup chopped dates
1/3 cup chopped dried apricots
1/3 cup chopped raisins
1/3 cup chopped dried cranberries

Apple juice as needed
1/3 cup chopped figs (optional)
1 cup chopped walnuts
1/4 cup chopped pistachio nuts
2 tbs. baking powder
2 tsp. baking soda
1/4 tsp. salt
1/2 tsp. cinnamon
1/4 tsp. nutmeg
1/4 tsp. ground cloves
1/4 tsp. allspice

Preheat the oven to 350°F.

Cream the sugars with the oil. Beat in one egg at a time with their shells. Stir in the pumpkin and applesauce, beating well. In another bowl, mix the dry ingredients. Slowly add to the wet mixture, beating well each time, making sure that it is well moistened before adding more dry ingredients.

SUBSTITUTION TIP: You can substitute safflower oil, sunflower oil, or walnut oil for vegetable oil.

Stir in dried apricots, cranberries, dates, figs, raisins, and nuts. Stir until well blended. Let it sit for 10-20 minutes. Stir once again. Spoon into greased muffin pan, loaf pan, or other shape pan. Bake between 20-60 minutes. (This depends on whether you use a pan, mini muffin pan, etc.) Use the toothpick test. If the toothpick comes out clean after sticking it into the center of the loaf, then it is done.

Allow to cool. My birds love it still slightly warm. I prefer using the smaller pans because they produce perfect, single servings for birds. This bread also freezes well.

Chili Pumpkin Cornbread

2 boxes of cornmeal mix
2 eggs with shells (washed)
Apple juice, as needed
$^1/_2$ cup Kaytee pellets, finely ground
1 canned pumpkin (16 oz.)
2 tbs. sesame seeds
2 tbs. dried vegetables

2 tbs. dried chili peppers
1 bag of mixed vegetables
1 package of instant oatmeal
1-2 tbs. oat groats
$^1/_2$ cup cooked kidney or lima beans
$^1/_2$ cup cottage cheese or plain
   yogurt

Preheat the oven to 350°F.

In a large bowl, mix all the dry ingredients. Add the eggs and pumpkin, mixing well. Add the other ingredients to the mix, stirring until well blended. Keep adding enough juice to make into a corn bread batter. Pour into a greased 9x13 pan or mini loafs and bake for 30-40 minutes or until a toothpick comes out clean. This can also be made into a muffin.

High Protein Muffins

10 oz. high-protein breeder pellets
1 cup of 15-bean mix, cooked
$^3/_4$ cup multi-grain flour
$^3/_4$ cup whole wheat flour
3 eggs plus shells
$^1/_2$ cup cornmeal
$^1/_2$ cup raw carrots chopped in
   blender

$^1/_2$ cup sunflower seeds
1 cup canned pumpkin
$^1/_2$ cup chopped broccoli
$^1/_2$ cup cooked mashed yams
Carrot juice, as needed

TIP: Chop up nuts ahead of time and store them in airtight containers. This way, you can use them whenever you need them.

Preheat the oven to 350°F.

Cover pellets with carrot juice to soften. Mash. Add all the dry ingredients to the softened pellets. Blend well. Puree the remaining ingredients; then add to the dry mixture. If needed, add more carrot juice. Bake for 35-45 minutes or until done. This is also rich in vitamin A and is great for weaning babies. Also excellent for breeders.

Chili Nut Muffins

2 cups Bisquick or other similar mix
1 cup cornmeal
$1/4$ cup chili powder (mild)
$1/4$ cup ground walnuts
1 cup water
2 eggs with shells (washed)

Preheat oven to 375°F.

Wash the eggs before you start. Mix all dry ingredients together first. Blend the eggs, shells included, with the water in a blender to be sure the shell is ground very fine. Add the water and eggs to the dry mix and stir, mixing well.

Grease and flour two 8x8-inch square cake pans. Divide the batter into the two pans and bake for about 35-45 minutes or until a toothpick comes out clean after being pushed into the center of the cake. Remove when done and turn onto cooling racks.

HELPFUL SUGGES-TION: Planting your own herb garden can be a useful resource—it does not require a lot of space, and you can grow many of the herbs used for seasonings.

When cool, cut into 1-inch squares and put back into the baking pans loosely. Then return the cubes to the oven at 150°F for about one hour to dry them more completely. This will help preserve the tiny cakes. After they have cooled, put into a plastic zip bag and refrigerate or freeze. This will keep in the refrigerator for up to a week (if the birds will let you).

The chili nut muffins smell great, and the birds will love them. I usually make them into muffins and bake for 30-35 minutes. Chili nut muffins are very spicy, but birds really love them.

Parrot Bread

1/3 cup vegetable oil or safflower oil
6 large eggs with shells (washed)
2-4 tbs. canned pumpkin
2 tbs. applesauce
1/2 cup of frozen vegetables
1/2 cup cooked lima or pinto beans
1/2 cup cooked rice, preferably
  brown
1/2 cup apple juice

2 cups cornmeal or 2 cornbread
  mixes
3-4 tbs. baking powder
1 cuttlebone or mineral block, finely
  ground
1/2 cup millet
1/2 cup Kaytee pellets
1/3 cup wheat germ oil
1 very ripe banana, mashed

Preheat the oven to 350°F.

Finely grind up the cuttlebone or mineral block first. Mix the millet, pellets, wheat germ oil, vegetable oil, banana, and cuttlebone in a food processor until they become finely blended. Add the eggs, pumpkin, and applesauce and continue to blend. Add the cooked beans and rice and lightly mix. Pour this mixture into a large bowl and add the cornmeal (or cornbread mix) and baking powder. Add the apple juice as needed if the mixture is too dry. Continue mixing until all ingredients are well blended and it has the consistency of cornbread. Pour the ingredients into a 9x13 pan or mini loaf pans. Bake for 30-40 minutes or until done. Serve warm with vitamins, minerals, or spirulina sprinkled on top. You can also make this in muffin pans.

Pelleted Birdie Bread

2 cups of Kaytee pellets
1/2 cup barley
1/2 cup oats
1/2 cup wheat flour
1 cup applesauce
1/2 cup mashed banana
1/4 cup brown sugar
4-5 large eggs with shells (washed)
1/2 cup fresh almond butter
2 tbs. baking powder

1 pinch each of nutmeg, cinnamon, and allspice
1/2 cup raisins
1/2 cup dried cranberries
1/2 cup finely chopped broccoli
1/2 cup frozen corn
1/2 cup frozen peas
1/2 cup mixed, unsalted, chopped nuts
1/2 cup finely chopped collard greens
1/2 cup carrot juice

Preheat oven to 375°F.

Thaw out frozen veggies. Mix all ingredients together. If too dry, add more carrot juice; if too wet, add more pellets. Bake in pan for 45-60 minutes or in muffin tins for 30-35 minutes. It is done when toothpick comes out clean or when the bread is pulling away from sides.

Fast and Easy Muffins

2 cups flour
1/2 cup oats
2 tbs. baking powder
2 eggs with shells (washed)

1 16 oz. can split pea soup
1/2 soup can of water
3 tbs. margarine

Preheat oven to 375°F.

Mix the dry ingredients together in a medium bowl. In another bowl, add the eggs, split pea soup, and melted margarine. Blend well. Pour the dry ingredients into the wet ingredients little by little, beating well each time.

Grease or line muffin tins. Pour into muffins. Bake for 20-30 minutes or until a toothpick comes out clean.

HELPFUL HINT: When using any soups in a recipe, use soups that are low in sodium.

Almond Muffins

1 large can of pumpkin
2 cups Cream of Wheat or Cream of
  Rice
2 cups grits
1 cup oatmeal
$1/2$ cup natural applesauce
1 large egg with shell (washed)

2 cups water or juice
3 tbs. baking powder
2 tbs. cinnamon
$1/2$ cup raisins or dried cranberries
$1/2$ cup sugar
1 tbs. vegetable oil
$1/2$ cup chopped almonds

SUBSTITUTION TIP:
For a different taste, try adding cranberry juice. When using juices, use ones that are 100-percent juice and without sugar added.

Preheat oven to 375°F.

This is a very heavy mixture. You can add more juice to make the batter not as thick. Mix all ingredients together, adding water, carrot juice, apple juice, or other juice. Line muffin tins with cupcake paper and fill $3/4$ of the way up. Bake 30-40 minutes or until a toothpick comes out clean. A heavier, thicker batter, these come out a little on the heavy side, but my birds enjoy them.

Broccoli Cheese Muffins

1 cup flour
1 cup multi-grain flour
2 tbs. baking powder
$1/4$ cup sugar
1 cup chopped broccoli (use the
  tops)
$1/4$ cup grated carrots
$1/4$ cup shredded cheddar cheese

1 tsp. ground nutmeg
1 tsp. salt
1 egg with shell (washed)
$1/2$ cup yogurt
1 cup milk
1 tsp. lemon juice
$1/4$ cup honey

Preheat oven to 375°F. Grease or line muffin tins.

In a large bowl, mix the flours together. Add the other dry ingredients and mix together. In another bowl, beat together the egg, yogurt, honey, milk, and lemon juice. Pour into the dry ingredients and mix well. Add the broccoli and carrots, mixing well. Bake for 35-40 minutes or until a toothpick comes out clean.

Pumpkin Apple Muffins

4 packages corn bread mix
1 package of frozen collard greens
4 eggs with shells (washed)
1 cup plain yogurt with live cultures
1-2 cups cooked squash, yams, or
   pumpkin

$^1/_2$ cup chopped apple
$^1/_2$ cup dried cranberries
$^1/_2$ cup fresh berries (if in season)
$^1/_2$ cup ground almonds
1 cup Kaytee pellets
Carrot juice as needed

Preheat oven to 375°F.

Blend yogurt, eggs, and greens until it becomes a liquid. Mix all the remaining ingredients. If the mixture is too dry, add carrot juice a little at a time until it has the consistency of cornbread. Bake for 35-45 minutes or until a toothpick comes out clean.

SUBSTITUTION TIP: If you can't find collard greens, use spinach or mustard greens instead.

Really Tasty Bread

1 cup cornmeal
$^1/_2$ cup whole wheat flour
$^1/_2$ cup rye flour
$^1/_4$ cup Cream of Rice
$^1/_4$ cup Malt-O-Meal
$^1/_4$ cup grits
$^1/_4$ rolled oats
4 tsp. baking powder
$^1/_2$ cup peanut butter
$^1/_4$ cup raisins

1 jar baby food squash (4 oz.)
1 jar baby food sweet potatoes (4 oz.)
1 jar baby food applesauce (4 oz.)
1 jar baby food carrots (4 oz.)
1 jar baby food spinach (4 oz.)
1 cup chopped broccoli
2 eggs with shells (washed)
$^1/_4$ cup grated cheddar cheese
1 cup puffed rice cereal
1 cup juice as needed

Preheat oven to 375°F.

Chop the broccoli in a food processor and add eggs and shells until the shells are ground. Add remaining ingredients, adding juice as needed. Pour (spread) in a 9x13 pan. Bake for 30-40 minutes or until toothpick comes out clean. Can also be baked into a muffin.

HELPFUL TIP: When using cuttlebone in any of these recipes, it is best to break it up into smaller pieces before grinding it up. To make this job easier, put the cuttlebone in a plastic bag and, using a hammer, you can pound it up into small pieces.

Tiny's Healthy Yum Bread

1 cup cornmeal
1/2 cup multi-grain flour
1/2 cup rye flour
1/3 cup oats
1/3 cup Cream of Rice
2 tsp. baking powder
1/2 cup almond butter or chunky
  peanut butter
1/4 cup mixed dried fruit

1 jar baby food carrots
1 jar baby food sweet potatoes (4 oz.)
1 jar baby food applesauce (4 oz.)
1/4 cup grated cheddar cheese
1 large carrot, chopped
1 cup chopped broccoli
2 eggs with shells (washed)
1 cup puffed brown rice cereal
Carrot juice

SUBSTITUION TIP: You can substitute kasha cereal for the puffed brown rice cereal. You can use any kind of juice you want. Try your health food store for a healthy selection.

Preheat oven to 375°F.

Chop carrots and broccoli in a food processor until finely chopped. Add eggs and shells and process for 30 seconds. Mix all the remaining ingredients together, adding juice as needed to make an easily spread consistency. Spread in a well greased and floured 9x13 pan and bake for 30-40 minutes or until done.

Mega Cornbread

3 cups corn muffin mix
4 eggs with shells (washed)
Water or juice as needed

1/2 cup mixed vegetables
1/4 cup chopped nuts
1/4 cup grated carrots

TIP: You can freeze any of these muffins and just take out what you need. I make up 2-3 batches of each. I then let them thaw to room temperature and put them in the microwave for 20 seconds to warm them up.

Preheat oven to 375°F.

Mix the first three ingredients in a bowl, beating until smooth. Stir in the mixed vegetables, chopped nuts, and carrots. Pour in a greased corn bread pan or in greased or lined muffin tins. Cook muffins for 30-35 minutes. Cook pan cornbread for 30-45 minutes or until toothpick comes out clean. Let cool. Slice into small pieces, put in plastic zip bags, and freeze until needed. Microwave to heat and serve. (Warm only—no hot spots!)

Butternut Squash Muffins

2 cups flour
2 tbs. sugar
1 tbs. baking powder
1 tsp. salt
1 egg with shell (washed)

1 cup milk
1/4 cup melted margarine
2/3 cup cooked mashed butternut
    squash
1/4 cup finely chopped carrots

Preheat the oven to 375°F.

Grease or line muffin pan. In a large bowl, mix the dry ingredients together. In a medium bowl, beat the egg, milk, melted margarine, squash, and carrots. Beat until blended. If the mixture is too wet, add more flour; if it's too dry, add more juice.

Pour into the dry ingredients, mixing well until all dry ingredients are moistened. Bake for 20-30 minutes or until done.

Cereal Birdie Bread

2 boxes muffin mix
3/4 cup Grapenuts cereal or similiar
    cereal
1/2 cup Cheerios cereal
1 cup dry oatmeal
1 tbs. palm nut oil

2 cups natural apple juice
2 eggs with shells (washed)
1 apple without skin, diced
1/4 cup light corn syrup
1/4 cup grated carrots
1 tbs. baking powder

Preheat oven to 350°F.

Grind all the cereals. Mix all dry ingredients. Add the wet ingredients, mixing well. If too dry, add more apple juice. Grease muffin pans. Pour into muffin pans and bake for 30 minutes or until a toothpick comes out clean. You can also pour

HELPFUL HINTS: You can use any type of nuts; however, almonds have higher calcium amounts.

the mix into a greased bread pan and bake for 40-45 minutes or until a toothpick comes out clean.

Cereal birdie bread is very tasty. My tiels especially enjoy it. Try adding extra carrots to this recipe for additional flavor.

Multi-grain Cheesy Apple Muffins

2 cups of multi-grain flour
1 1/2 tsp. baking powder
1/2 tsp. baking soda
1 tsp. salt
1/4 cup sugar
1/2 cup margarine, softened

1 cup apple juice
1/2 cup shredded cheese
2 eggs with shells (washed)
1/2 cup chopped apple
1/2 cup shredded carrots
1/4 cup chopped walnuts

Preheat oven to 350°F.

Mix first five ingredients together. Put the eggs with washed shells into the blender. Process until the shells are finely ground. Next, add the margarine, sugar, apple, carrots, and walnuts. Blend briefly. Add this to the dry ingredients and stir until combined. Spoon mix into greased muffin tins and bake for 30-35 minutes or until toothpick comes out clean.

Orange Nutty Muffins

2 cups whole wheat flour
1 cup ground Kaytee pellets
3 cups orange juice
6 eggs with shells
2 very ripe bananas, mashed
1 cup pellets (cockatiel size)
1 cup oatmeal

1/2 cup powdered milk
3 tbs. baking powder
1 cup chopped mixed nuts
  (unsalted)
1/3 cup wheat germ oil
Water

FOOD FACT: There is a difference between sweet potatoes and yams. Yams contain 1 1/2 times the amount of vitamin A than that of the sweet potato. They also have twice the amount of calcium.

Preheat oven to 350°F.

Mix the ground pellets, whole wheat flour, powdered milk, baking powder, and oatmeal in a large bowl. Add the eggs, orange juice, oil, and mashed bananas, mixing well. Stir in mixed nuts and cockatiel-size pellets.

Line muffin tins with paper and fill almost to the top. Bake for 35-45 minutes or until a toothpick comes out clean. Cool. Remove paper before giving to your bird. To make as a bread instead of muffins, you can also pour into greased 9x13 pan and bake for 55-60 minutes or until toothpick comes out clean. Cool.

Zucchini Corn Muffins

2 boxes corn muffin mix
4 eggs with shells (washed)
$1/2$ cup milk
$1/2$ cup raisins
$1/2$ cup cranberries (fresh, if
   possible)

1 cup diced apples
1 cup grated carrots
1 cup grated zucchini
$1/4$ cup pine nuts

Preheat oven to 350°F.

Mix the first five ingredients together in a large bowl, mixing well. Add the remaining ingredients, mixing well each time. If too dry, add more milk. Grease and flour two bread pans or muffin pans. Bake for 30-45 minutes or until done. (If using muffin pans, baking time is less; if using bread pans, time may be more.)

HELPFUL HINT: If you don't have fresh vegetables available, you can substitute frozen

Toby's Favorite Muffins

2 boxes of corn bread mix
2 tbs. baking powder
1 tsp. spirulina
1 tsp. bee pollen granules
2 eggs with shells
2 small jars baby food (4 oz. each)
$3/4$ cup nut butter
2 cups baby cereal

$1/2$ cup grated carrots
$1/2$ cup grated zucchini
$1/2$ cup grated sweet potatoes (yams)
Carrot juice as needed
$1/4$ cup pureed bananas
$1/4$ cup pureed papaya
$1/4$ cup chopped pine nuts
3 tbs. coconut milk

Preheat oven to 375°F.

Warning: This is a very heavy batter and is hard to mix.

Mix together ingredients. If the mixture is too dry, add carrot juice a little at a time. Grease and flour a 9x13 pan and pour mixture into pan. Bake for 30-40 minutes or until done. Cool and cut into small birdie-size squares. This can be frozen.

This recipe is especially good for birds who are extremely thin. I use coconut milk because it is high in fat, providing more calories, and I use papaya because it is good for digestion. I use almond butter because it's higher in calcium, and I use yams because they are higher in vitamin A.

Veggie Pellet Bread

2 cups Kaytee pellets, crumbled
1 banana
6 eggs with shells (washed)
6 tbs. canned pumpkin
1/3 cup oil
1/2 cup applesauce

1 cup mixed vegetables
1 cup cooked 15-bean mix
1 cup cooked brown rice
2 cups cornmeal
2 tbs. baking powder
Carrot juice as needed

Preheat oven to 350°F.

In a food processor, add the pellets, banana, eggs with shells, pumpkin, oil, applesauce, and vegetables. Process until well mixed. Add the rice and 15-bean mix and blend until pulverized.

Next, add the corn meal and the baking powder. If the mixture is too dry or too thick, add some carrot juice. Pour into a greased pan and bake for 40-50 minutes or until a toothpick comes out clean.

Green Muffins

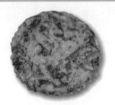

1 box corn bread muffin mix
1 egg with shell (washed)
1 large carrot (tops okay)
1 small yam, cooked

1 very ripe banana
1 handful of dandelion greens
1/2 tsp. cayenne pepper
Water or juice

CAUTION: Dandelion greens are very nutritious, but if you use dandelion greens, make sure they are from a lawn that is untreated. You can always substitute mustard greens, spinach, or broccoli for the dandelion greens if untreated dandelion greens cannot be found.

Preheat oven to 350°F.

In a food processor, add all the ingredients, adding water or fruit juice as needed. Bake in a greased or lined muffin pan around 30-35 minutes or until a toothpick comes out clean. The final product will be slightly green in color.

Bean and Rice Muffins

1/3 cup vegetable oil or safflower oil
6 large eggs with shells
2-4 tbs. canned pumpkin
2 tbs. applesauce
1 cup of frozen vegetables
1 cup cooked mixed beans
1 cup cooked rice, preferably brown
1 cup cornmeal or cornbread mix

3-4 tbs. baking powder
1 cuttlebone or mineral block, finely ground
1 cup millet
1 cup Kaytee pellets
1/3 cup wheat germ oil
1 very ripe banana

Preheat the oven to 325°F.

Mix the seed, pellets, wheat germ oil, vegetable oil, banana, and ground cuttlebone or mineral block in a food processor until it becomes finely blended. Add the eggs, pumpkin, and applesauce and continue to blend. Add the cooked beans and rice and lightly mix.

Pour this mixture into a large bowl and add the cornmeal and baking powder. If the mixture is too dry, you can add more canned pumpkin or applesauce. Continue mixing until all ingredients are well blended and it has the consistency of cornbread. Pour the ingredients into a 9x13 pan or mini-loaf pan. You can also make into muffins. Bake for 30-40 minutes or until done. Serve warm with vitamins, minerals, or spirulina sprinkled on top.

Miller's Favorite Muffins

2 cups of canned pumpkin
2 cups Cream of Wheat
2 cups of oatmeal
1/2 -1 cup of natural applesauce
1 egg with shell
1 tsp. baking powder
Apple juice, as needed

2 tbs. cinnamon
1/4 cup raisins
1/4 cup mixed dried fruit
1/4 cup sugar
2 tsp. sesame seeds
1 tsp. walnut oil

Preheat oven to 375°F.

Mix all ingredients together, adjusting the applesauce, adding more if too dry. (Or you can add apple juice instead.) Add more oatmeal if too wet. Pour into greased muffin pan and bake for 20-30 minutes or until done.

Rainforest Muffins

2 cups whole wheat
$1/3$ cup wheat germ
2 eggs with shells (washed)
1 tbs. baking powder
1 tbs. palm oil
2 tbs. palm nut pulp
1 cup fresh coconut
2 $1/2$ cups papaya juice
1 tsp. bee pollen

$1/2$ cup Brazil nuts
$1/4$ cup almonds
$1/4$ cup walnuts
$1/2$ cup macadamia nuts
1 cup mixed dried fruit
$1/2$ cup banana chips
1 mashed banana
$1/4$ cup nut butter

TIP: Whenever you use nuts in any recipe, use unsalted nuts. Also use human-grade nuts. Always store nuts properly to prevent mold.

Preheat oven to 350°F.

In a large bowl, mix all of the whole wheat flour, wheat germ, bee pollen, and baking powder together. Add the eggs, palm oil, palm nut pulp, coconut, nut butter, and papaya juice. In a food processor, chop up the nuts and banana chips. Add this to the other mixture, mixing until well blended. Spoon into greased muffin tins or ones that are lined. Bake for 35-40 minutes or until a toothpick comes out clean.

Birdie Super Bread

2 boxes of corn bread mix
2 large eggs with shells (washed)
3 very ripe bananas, mashed
1 cup mini pellets, ground

$1/2$ cup coarse ground walnuts
$1/2$ cup frozen vegetables
1 cup of apple juice

HELPFUL TIP: Use cupcake liners to line the muffin trays. This makes for an easier cleanup. You will no longer have the need to grease the muffin trays.

Preheat oven to 375°F.

Mix all of the dry ingredients together. Add the eggs, mashed bananas, and vegetables, adjusting the apple juice as needed, and pour into a pan sprayed with nonstick vegetable spray. Bake for 35 to 45 minutes or until a toothpick comes out clean. Once cooled, cut into serving-size squares for your individual birds. Refrigerate up to three days. Can also be frozen.

Rocky's Favorite Muffins

2 boxes corn muffin mix
2 eggs with shells
$2/3$ cup papaya juice
4 large yams, boiled and mashed
1 Granny Smith apple
2 bananas, mashed

$1/2$ cup mixed dried fruit
$1/4$-$1/3$ cup almond butter
1 tsp. cinnamon
1 cup of any flavor of Crazy Corn
1 tbs. bee pollen

Preheat oven to 450°F.

Prepare Crazy Corn according to instructions. Peel and core the apple, cutting it into small pieces. Mix all ingredients together, adding more liquid if needed. Grease a 9x13 pan. Bake for 35-45 minutes or until a toothpick comes out clean. Once cooled, cut into squares and serve.

HELPFUL HINT: When using apples, alway peel and core first . Remember that the seeds inside are toxic to birds.

Yummy Muffins

I found this recipe in one of my cookbooks and have adapted it for my birds. I have made it an excellent source for calcium and vitamin A. They really love it.

4 boxes of corn bread mix
4 bottles of baby banana/yogurt juice (4 oz.)
$1/4$ cup pureed papayas
$1/4$ cup cooked sweet potatoes, mashed

$1/4$ cup canned pumpkin
$1/2$ cup pureed macaroni and cheese
1 cup applesauce, chunky-natural
$1/4$ cup pureed carrots
$1/2$ finely chopped almonds
1 tsp bee pollen granules

Preheat oven to 350°F.

Reserve $1/2$ cup of applesauce and $1/4$ cup of almonds. Mix ingredients together, adding more juice as needed. Grease and flour muffin pans and pour ingredients in pans. Top with apple-sauce and almonds and bake for 25-35 minutes or until done.

Apple Date Muffins

1 1/2 cups whole wheat flour
1/4 cup bran cereal
3/4 cup chopped apple (peeled, cored)
1/4 cup chopped dates
1/2 cup walnuts (chopped)
1/4 cup honey

1 tsp. bee pollen
1 tsp. wheat germ
2 tsp. baking powder
1/4 tsp. salt
1/2 tsp. cinnamon
2 large eggs with shells (washed)
3/4 cup milk

Preheat oven to 375°F.

Grease or line muffin tins. In a large bowl, mix together the flour, bran cereal, baking powder, bee pollen, wheat germ, salt, cinnamon, apples, dates, and walnuts. In a smaller bowl, beat eggs. Beat in the milk and honey. Pour this mixture into the large bowl and blend until all ingredients are well moistened. Bake for 30-40 minutes or until a toothpick comes out clean.

Applesauce Oatmeal Muffins

1 1/4 cups flour
1 1/2 cups quick cooking oats
1/2 tsp. baking powder
1/2 tsp. baking soda
1 tsp. ground nutmeg
1 tsp. ground cinnamon
1 tsp. allspice
1 tsp. wheat germ

1/2 cup walnuts
1/2 cup pecans
4 egg whites
1/3 cup margarine
1/2 cup brown sugar
1 cup chunky applesauce
1/2 cup raisins (optional)
Juice, as needed

Preheat oven to 375°F.

SUBSTITUTION HINT:
Try using the different flavored applesauces. My birds love apple-berry flavored applesauce.

Grease or line muffin pan. In a large bowl, blend the flour, oats, baking powder, baking soda, nutmeg, wheat germ, cinnamon, allspice, walnuts, and pecans. In a small bowl, beat egg whites until foamy. Beat in sugar and butter. Stir in the applesauce. Mix the two bowls together until well moistened. I add raisins to this occasionally, and my birds love it. Bake for 30-35 minutes or until a toothpick comes out clean. This is a moist muffin.

Apple Veggie Muffins

2 1/2 cups flour
2 tbs. baking powder
2 tsp. baking soda
1 tsp. wheat germ
1 tsp. cinnamon
1/2 cup sugar
2 cups finely chopped apples
1 cup finely chopped cranberries
3/4 cup finely shredded carrots

3/4 cup finely shredded zucchini
1 cup chopped almonds
1 tbs. crushed mineral block
1/2 tsp. salt
2 large eggs
1/2 cup oil
1 1/2 cups juice

Preheat oven to 375°F.

Grease or line muffin tins. In a large bowl, mix together the flour, sugar, baking powder, salt, cinnamon, mineral block, baking soda, and wheat germ. When mixed, add the apples, cranberries, carrots, zucchini, and almonds. In another bowl, mix the eggs thoroughly. Add the oil and juice, mixing well. Pour into the dry ingredients and mix until well moistened. Bake for 25-30 minutes or until a toothpick comes out clean.

Spicy-Hot Corn Muffins

1 1/2 cups corn flour
1/2 cup flour
2 tsp. baking powder
1 tsp salt
2 large eggs with shells

1 cup milk
1 tbs. margarine
3 tbs. finely chopped jalapeno
    peppers

Preheat oven to 375°F.

In a large bowl, mix the corn flour, flour, baking powder, and salt. In a medium bowl, mix the eggs until foamy. Add the milk and melted margarine and beat well. Add the jalapeno peppers. Pour into the dry ingredients and mix well. Grease or line muffin tin and pour in ingredients. Bake for 25-30 minute or until a toothpick comes out clean. (Warning: These are spicy hot!)

HELPFUL HINT:
Because many recipes call for ground mineral blocks or cuttlebones, grind up an entire batch. Store in an airtight container or plastic zip bag.

Tomato Muffins

$^3/_4$ cup flour
1 cup whole wheat flour
1 tbs. baking powder
$^1/_4$ cup sugar
1 large egg with shell (washed)
$^1/_4$ cup walnut oil

$^1/_4$ cup milk
1 can tomato soup
3 tbs. Parmesan cheese
$^1/_4$ tsp. fresh basil
$^1/_2$ tsp. garlic
$^1/_2$ cup chopped spinach

HELPFUL HINT:
Choose a tomato soup
that is low in sodium.
Birds do not need the
extra salt content.

Preheat oven to 375°F.

Grease or line muffin tins. In a large bowl, blend all the dry ingredients together. In a medium bowl, beat egg. Beat in the oil, milk, and soup. Pour into the dry ingredients and mix well. Add the chopped spinach, mixing until it is well blended. Bake for 25-30 minutes or until done.

Chicken, Rice, and Tomato Muffins

2 cups finely chopped cooked
    chicken
2 cups flour
1 cup cooked rice
1 tbs. baking powder
1 tsp. garlic powder
1 tsp. wheat germ

1 tsp. salt
2 large eggs with shells (washed)
$^1/_4$ tsp. mustard powder
$^1/_4$ cup vegetable oil
1 can tomato soup
1 tbs. tomato paste
1 pinch of pepper

Preheat oven to 375°F.

Lightly grease or line muffin tins. In a large bowl, blend together all dry ingredients. In a medium bowl, beat eggs. Mix the oil, tomato soup, and tomato paste in. Add to the dry ingredients, mixing well. Add the cooked chicken and cooked rice, mixing until well blended. Bake for 30-35 minutes or until a toothpick comes out clean.

You can make this into a Mexican chicken, rice, and tomato recipe by substituting salsa for the tomato soup and adding chopped jalapeno peppers.

I use the leftover rice from the rice stuffing recipes for these muffins.

Layered Muffins

This is a very different type of muffin. This muffin has three different layers, not including the toppings. It takes more time to make these, but my birds enjoy them, and I'm sure yours will, too.

Batter
1 cup flour
$1/2$ cup whole wheat flour
$1/2$ cup corn flour
1 tbs. baking powder
1 tsp. salt
2 large eggs with shells
$1/2$ cup oil
1 cup milk
$1/2$ tsp hot sauce

First Layer
$1/2$ cup finely chopped broccoli
1 tbs. Parmesan cheese
Second Layer
$1/2$ cup corn (well drained)
$1/4$ tsp. garlic powder
Third Layer
$1/2$ cup thinly sliced zucchini
1 tbs. Romano cheese
Topping
$1/4$ cup shredded carrots
$1/4$ tsp. garlic powder
$1/4$ cup chopped walnuts

Preheat oven to 375°F.

For the batter, in a large bowl, mix together the flour, whole wheat flour, and the corn flour. Then, add the baking powder and the salt. In a medium bowl, beat the eggs. Gradually add in the milk, oil, and hot sauce. Add to the dry ingredients and mix well.

You will need four separate bowls for the next steps. In one bowl, add the broccoli and cheese; in another bowl add the corn and garlic powder. In the third bowl, add the zucchini and cheese, and in the last one, add the carrots, garlic powder, and walnuts.

SUBSTITION HINT: Try substituting raw pumpkin seeds for the walnuts

Divide the batter evenly in the first three bowls, mixing well each time. Grease or line muffin tins. Using a tablespoon, drop 1 tbs. of the broccoli and cheese batter into the greased or lined muffin tin. Once done, repeat with the corn and garlic powder mix. Finish with the zucchini and garlic mix. Sprinkle the tops of the muffins with the carrots, garlic powder, and walnuts. Bake for 30-35 minutes or until a toothpick comes out clean.

Nutty Muffins

3 cups flour
1/2 cup sugar
4 tbs. baking powder
1/4 cup pine nuts, chopped
1/4 cup pecans, chopped
1/4 cup walnuts, chopped
1/4 cup pistachios, chopped
1/4 cup Brazil nuts, chopped
1/4 cup hazelnuts (filberts)

1/4 cup peanuts, chopped
1/4 cup almonds, chopped
1/4 cup macadamia nuts, chopped
1/4 cup raw sunflower seeds
1/4 cup raw pumpkin seeds
2 large eggs with shells (washed)
1 cup milk
1/2 cup margarine, melted

HELPFUL HINT: If your bird is on the thin side, add more nuts to the muffins. Nuts are high in fat. Always make sure nuts are mold-free and fresh. Do not use nuts that are webby inside.

Preheat oven to 375°F.

In a large bowl, mix together the flour, sugar, and baking powder. In a medium bowl, beat eggs. Beat in the milk and melted margarine. Pour into the dry ingredients, mixing until well moistened. Gradually add the nuts, one type at a time, mixing well.

When all the nuts and seeds are added, you will have a very heavy batter that will be very thick with nuts. In fact, it will mainly look like nuts. Grease or line muffin tins. Spoon into the tins. Bake 30-35 minutes or until done.

Nutty muffins are a favorite of all my birds. I make this on special occassions.

South of the Border Muffins

1 can of Southwestern corn bread
  mix
8 oz. jar of salsa

2 jalapeno peppers, chopped
1 zucchini, grated
1 can creamed corn

SUBSTITUTION TIP: For something different, use different kinds of salsa. I use pineapple salsa, mango salsa, etc. Check out the salsa aisle at your grocery store. There are many different types available.

Preheat oven to 350°F.

In a large bowl, combine the salsa, jalapeno peppers, zucchini, and creamed corn, mixing well. Add the corn bread mix, stirring until well blended. If too dry, add water. Bake in greased or lined muffin tins for 30-40 minutes or until a toothpick comes out dry.

South of the Border Muffins have a very interesting taste. Your bird will really enjoy it.

Cornbread Deluxe

1 large box of cornbread muffin mix
1 canned pumpkin
1 cup mixed vegetables

Preheat oven to 350°F.

Mix corn bread according to instructions, and then add the pumpkin and mixed veggies. Pour into muffin tins. (You can also use a 9x13 pan). Because of the pumpkin and vegetables, it needs around five minutes more cooking time than the instructions call for. I have found 35-40 minutes is best for muffins and 45-60 minutes for the pan.

When cooled, you can cut into small squares or just hand out the muffins. This freezes well. You can also add other things, such as chopped nuts. Birds go crazy over this.

Beta-Carotene Muffins

2 boxes of muffin mix
1 cup shredded carrots
1 large yam, boiled, mashed
$1/2$-1 can pumpkin (small can)

$1/2$ cup palm nut pulp
$1/4$ cup nuts, chopped
$1/4$ cup carrot juice
Water from yam

Preheat oven to 375°F.

Scrub the yam thoroughly. Cut into quarters. In a small pot, add enough water to cover the yam and boil. It is easier to remove the skins when you boil with the skin on. Remove the skins when done and set water aside; then mash the yam.

In a large bowl, add the shredded carrots, mashed yams, pumpkin, palm nut pulp, and nuts. Mix well. Add the muffin mix to this, stirring well. Add the carrot juice, mixing well. If it is still too dry, add the water from the boiled yam or more carrot juice.

When the mixture has the consistency of cornbread, pour into greased or lined muffin tin. Bake for 30 minutes or until a toothpick comes out clean.

Beta-carotene muffins are a great way to give your bird extra vitamin A.

Bean, Lentil, and Squash Spicy Loaf

2 tsp. peanut oil or olive oil
2 ribs of celery, chopped
1¹/₂ cups of mixed cooked beans
¹/₂ cup of cooked lentils
2 eggs, well beaten, with shells
  (washed)
2 large carrots, finely chopped

1 cup of cooked squash, any variety
¹/₂ cup cheddar cheese (or any
  variety)
1 cup whole wheat bread crumbs
1-2 tsp. chili peppers or dried,
  crushed chili peppers
1 pinch of salt and pepper

Preheat oven to 350°F. Grease a loaf pan thoroughly.

In a sauce pan, add the oil, and when hot, add the celery. Cook until tender. Cut the cooked squash into small pieces and add to the celery. Cook for a few more minutes on medium heat. Allow it to cool. If you haven't rinsed the beans and lentils, do that now.

SAFETY TIP: Whenever you use beans of any kind, they must be cooked properly. Never feed raw beans to your birds. You can, however, feed sprouted beans.

In a food processor, add the rinsed and cooked beans and lentils. Process until smooth. Add the cooled celery and squash to the beans and lentils. Process another minute or two until smooth once again.

In a large bowl, add this mixture. Slowly add the eggs one at a time and mix well. Add the bread crumbs and the cheese. Mix well once again. Add the remaining ingredients, mixing well each time.

Spoon this mixture into the greased loaf pan and bake 1 hour or until firm to the touch. It will still be moist inside. Wait approximately one hour and serve.

Nutty Squash Loaf

1 tbs. oil (peanut, walnut, or olive)
2 celery ribs, finely chopped
1 to 1½ cups cooked lentils, rinsed and drained
1 to 1½ cups mixed nuts, finely chopped, no salt (I use almonds, pine nuts, and pistachios for this recipe)
½ cup whole wheat or multi-grain flour

½ cup cheddar cheese (you can also use Colby-Jack or other)
2 eggs, well beaten, with shells (washed)
1 cup mixed, cooked squash (I used spaghetti squash, acorn squash, and butternut squash)
1 pinch of salt and pepper
1 teaspoon of mixed herbs (your bird's favorites)

Preheat the oven to 375°F.

Thoroughly grease a loaf pan. Heat the oil in a large frying pan. Add the celery and the squash and cook until the celery is tender. While this is cooking, finely chop the nuts. Add the nuts, lentils, cheese, and flour to the frying pan. Turn the heat off. Mix thoroughly, blending well. Add the herbs and the salt and pepper. Continue mixing. Spoon mixture into the greased loaf pans. Cook around 1 hour or until firm to touch and the top is golden brown. Cut into slices and serve warm. (It will still be moist inside.)

You can substitute Monterey Jack cheese for Cheddar Cheese in most recipes.

Eclectus Birdie Bread

2 cups yellow corn meal
1 cup whole wheat flour
1 cup raisins or currants
1 cup nuts, chopped
1 cup shelled raw sunflower seeds

1 can pumpkin
1 cup papaya nectar
½ cup safflower oil
1 tsp. cinnamon
1 tbs. baking powder

Preheat oven to 350°F.

Mix all ingredients together. Add water if the mixture is too dry or more corn meal if it is too thin. Pour into greased or lined muffin tins. Bake for around 35-40 minutes or until toothpick comes out clean. This is a heavy muffin.

HELPFUL FACT: Remember—if it is good for you it is probably good for your bird. Food that is unsalted or has no sugar or preservatives is much healthier. Never feed avocados, rhubarb, or chocolate.

Cheesy Apple Muffins

2 cups whole wheat flour
2 tsp. baking powder
1 tsp. baking soda
1 tsp. salt
$^1/_3$ cup sugar
$^1/_2$ cup margarine, melted

$^1/_2$ cup shredded cheddar cheese
2 eggs with shells (washed)
$^3/_4$ cup chopped apple
$^1/_2$ cup shredded carrot
1 cup apple juice

SUBSTITUTION TIP:
For a change, substitute
carrot juice for the apple
juice. Carrot juice is
higher in vitamin A than
apple juice is.

Preheat oven to 350°F.

In a food processor, mix the first five ingredients together. Add eggs with the shells, mixing well. Add remaining ingredients and mix until well blended.

Spoon into lined muffin tins and bake for 30-35 minutes or until toothpick comes out clean.

Blueberry Almond Muffins

1 cup blueberries
$^1/_2$ cup chopped almonds
1 $^1/_4$ cups flour
1 cup whole wheat flour
1 cup yogurt
4 eggs with shells (washed)

2 tbs. margarine
$^1/_2$ cup sugar
1 tsp. baking soda
1 tbs. baking powder
1 pinch of salt

Preheat oven to 375°F.

In a large bowl, blend in flour, baking soda, baking powder, and salt. In another bowl, beat together the eggs, yogurt, sugar, and margarine. Mix two bowls together. Mix until well blended.

Fold in the blueberries and the almonds. Spoon the mixture into the greased or lined muffin tins. Bake for 30-35 minutes or until done.

HELPFUL HINT: When
using yogurt in any
recipe, always use
yogurt with live cultures.

Veggie Bread

2 cups finely ground Kaytee pellets
2 cups corn meal
4 tbs. baking powder
1 cuttlebone, finely ground
$1/3$ cup wheat germ oil
$1/3$ cup vegetable oil
6 large eggs with shells (washed)
Water or juice

$1/2$ can of canned pumpkin
1 tbs. applesauce
2 very ripe bananas, mashed
1 small bag mixed vegetables
1 cup of cooked 15-bean mix
1 cup brown rice, cooked
1 small zucchini, shredded

Preheat oven to 375°F.

In a food processor, mix the first four ingredients until you have a fine blend. Add the next three to four ingredients and continue blending. You should be able to pour the mixture; if you cannot, add more water or juice. Pour the mixture into a large bowl and add the rest of the ingredients. If it is still too dry, add more water or juice until you have reached the right consistency.

Pour into a greased 9x13 pan and bake 35-40 minutes or until a toothpick comes out clean. You can sprinkle with vitamins, wheat grass powder, and/or spirulina on warm bread and serve.

Banana Nut Wheat Muffins

2 cups whole wheat flour
$1/2$ cup sugar
1 tsp. baking powder
1 tsp. baking soda
$1/4$ tsp. salt

$3/4$ cup mashed bananas
$1/2$ cup chopped nuts
2 eggs with shells
$1/2$ cup vegetable oil
Water

Preheat oven to 375°F.

Mix all the dry ingredients together in a large bowl. In a food processor, mix eggs, oil, and bananas together. Add the dry ingredients and continue to process for a minute more. Add water if needed. Spoon mixture into lined muffin cups. Bake for 30-35 minutes or until a toothpick comes out clean.

Great Taste Bread

1 cup Kaytee pellets, ground into a powder
2 boxes corn bread mix
1/2 tsp. spirulina
1 can pumpkin
1 pinch of cinnamon
1 tsp. peanut butter
1 egg with shell (washed)
1/2 tsp. scraped cuttlebone or mineral block
1/2 cup finely chopped spinach
1/2 cup chopped chili peppers
Apple juice, as needed
1/2 cup mixed vegetables
1 pkg. instant flavored oatmeal
1/2 cup oat groats
1/2 cup frozen blueberries
1/4 cup raisins
1/4 cup dried cranberries
1/2 cup cooked 15-bean mix
1/2 cup cooked brown rice
1 small container any flavor yogurt
1/4 cup grated cheese

INTERESTING FACT: Birds have only 5 to 10 percent of the taste buds that people have. This is why they can eat all those hot, spicy peppers without any problems.

Preheat oven to 350°F.

In a large bowl, add all the dry ingredients. Add the egg, pumpkin, and yogurt, mixing well. Mix enough apple juice to make a corn bread-consistency batter. Mix all the remaining ingredients together.

Pour into one (or two) greased 9x13 baking pans. (You may want to make them thicker or thinner depending on your bird's desire.) Bake in a 350 degree oven about 40 minutes or until a toothpick comes out clean. If making thinner bread, cooking time is around 25-30 minutes.

You can also make into muffins. Bake for 30-40 minutes. Cool and cut into squares just the right size for your bird. Freeze all but one day's supply. When thawing, microwave until slightly warm.

Basic Birdie Bread

2 boxes corn muffin mix
1 tsp. spirulina
1 tbs. bee pollen
2 eggs with shells (washed)
Juice, as needed

4 jars of baby food (mixed, your
   choice)
1/2 cup peanut butter
1/4 cup chopped peanuts
1-2 cups chopped vegetables

Preheat oven to 375°F.

Mix all the ingredients together. If too dry, add more apple juice. Pour into a 9x13 greased pan and bake for 40-45 minutes. Cool and cut into individual squares. This can be frozen. This can also be made into a muffin. Bake for 30-35 minutes.

SUBSTITUTION TIP: You can substitute almond butter for the peanut butter in all of these recipes. Almonds are higher in calcium than other nuts.

The Breakfast Foods

Contents

Polly Biscuits

1 cup uncooked oatmeal
$^3/_4$ cup powdered milk
$^1/_3$ cup butter
$^1/_2$ cup cornmeal

1 tsp. vegetable bouillon
1 egg, beaten, with shell (washed)
$1^1/_2$ cup hot water
$3^1/_2$ cups multigrain flour

Preheat oven to 325°F.

In a large bowl, pour hot water over the oatmeal, butter, and bouillon. Let it stand about 5 minutes. Stir in the powdered milk, cornmeal, and the egg. Add flour, $^1/_2$ cup at a time, mixing well after each addition. Knead 5-7 minutes, adding more flour if necessary to make a very stiff dough. Roll out on a floured board to $^1/_2$-inch thickness and cut into shapes with any cookie cutter. Bake for about 35-50 minutes. Allow to cool and place on wire rack to totally dry before storing. This makes about 1 to $1^1/_2$ lbs.

Birdie Breakfast

3 oz. instant oatmeal
3 oz. GrapeNuts
1 cup evaporated skim milk
1 cup applesauce (no sugar added)
$^1/_2$ cup unsalted mixed nuts,
   chopped

$^1/_4$ cup raisins
$^1/_4$ cup chopped dried fruit mix
$^1/_4$ cup brown sugar
1 tsp. cinnamon
1 tsp. baking soda
1 cuttlebone, finely ground

Preheat oven to 350°F.

In a large bowl, mix all the ingredients. Add water if it is too dry. Pour into a greased 9x13 pan. Bake for 30 minutes or until toothpick comes out clean. Cool. Cut into the bars the appropriate size for your bird. Place the remaining bars into baggies and freeze.

HINT: Try the flavored oatmeals with fruit added.

This is really a very yummy treat; all my birds love it.

Carrot Pancakes

2 large eggs with shells (washed)
1/2 cup milk
1/4 cup melted margarine
2 tsp sugar

2 1/4 cups flour
3/4 cup finely chopped carrots
1 tbs. baking powder
1 tsp. wheat germ

Preheat a skillet or griddle. In a blender, mix the eggs, milk, margarine, salt, and sugar on high for 10 seconds. Add the flour, baking powder, and carrots and mix on high for 15 seconds or until smooth. Drop a

spoonful of batter onto the hot griddle. When the top looks dry, flip over. When golden brown on the other side, transfer to plate. Repeat with remaining batter. When cooled, give to your bird.

Healthy and easy to make, these pancakes are another great treat for your bird.

TIP: You can also make this using sweet potatoes instead of carrots.

Apple Waffles

1 1/2 cups flour
1 tsp. sugar
1 tbs. baking powder
1 apple, finely chopped (peeled, cored)

1/4 tsp. cinnamon
1/4 tsp. salt
2 eggs
1 cup milk
1/4 cup melted margarine

Preheat a waffle iron and prepare as directed. In a bowl, mix the flour, sugar, baking powder, apple, cinnamon, and salt. With a mixer, mix the eggs until foamy and add the milk and the melted margarine. Pour the wet ingredients into the dry ingredients, beating until smooth.

Pour a 1/2 cup of the batter onto the waffle iron and prepare according to manufacturer's instructions. Remove, and repeat with remaining batter. Serve slightly warm, not hot.

SUBSTITION HINTS: Waffles are a great way to get your bird to eat new foods. You can add any kind of berry or nuts to them. Try substituting pear for the apple for a different taste.

Banana French Toast

2 large eggs
1 medium banana, mashed
4 slices multi-grain bread

Mix eggs. Mash the banana and add into egg mixture. Dip bread into mixture. (Add water if needed.) In a frying pan sprayed with a nonstick spray, cook until both sides a golden brown. Cut into small pieces. Top with crushed almonds if preferred.

Waffle Treats

1 waffle mix
1 chopped apple
1 tsp. bee pollen
1 tsp. birdie vitamins

Tip: Try using fresh blueberries, strawberries, or mashed bananas in place of the apple.

Make mix according to instructions. Add the fresh fruit, bee pollen, and vitamins. Freeze any leftovers. They can be heated in the toaster anytime.

Quicky Breakfast

1 pack of instant oatmeal, any flavor
1 tsp. pine nuts, chopped
1-2 tbs. applesauce

TIP: Sprinkle Grape-Nuts on top for a special treat.

Cook oatmeal according to directions. Add the pine nuts and applesauce, mixing well. Let cool. This is also a good place to add vitamins, calcium, spirulina, wheatgrass, etc.

For those of you who have very little time in the morning, this is a fast and easy breakfast to make for your birds.

Blueberry Banana Waffles

2 cups flour
1 tbs. sugar
1/2 tsp. salt
3 tsp. baking powder
3 large eggs

1 1/2 cups milk
1/2 cup oil
1 cup mashed ripe bananas
1/2 cup fresh blueberries

Preheat a waffle iron and prepare according to manufacturer's instructions.

In a large bowl, combine the flour, sugar, baking powder, and salt. In a medium bowl, beat the eggs with an electric mixer until foamy. Add the milk, oil, and bananas. Mix well. Pour into dry ingredients and mix until smooth. Fold in the blueberries.

Pour half of the batter onto the waffle iron, and cook until done. Pour the remaining batter and repeat. Serve slightly warm, not hot.

HELPFUL HINT: You can make several batches at a time and freeze them. When you want more, just pop them into your toaster.

A great recipe for people, too!

Good Stuff Waffles

1 waffle mix
1/4 cup blueberries, chopped
1/4 cup strawberries, chopped
1/4 cup banana, mashed

1/4 cup apple, chopped
1/4 cup pecans, chopped
2 tbs. palm nut pulp (optional)

Prepare the waffle mix according to manufacturer's instructions. Add the chopped blueberries, strawberries, apple, and the mashed banana. Stir well. Add the pecans and the palm nut pulp, stirring until the mixture is well blended. Prepare a waffle iron and cook until a golden brown.

Birdie Cereal

TIP: Use low-sugar, low-salt cereals for your birds. It is much healthier.

1 cup granola
1/2 cup fruit bits or raisins
1/2 cup Cheerios
1/2 cup Chex (optional)

Mix all ingredients together.

Yam French Toast

2 eggs
1 medium yam, boiled and then pureed
4 slices of whole wheat toast

Mix the eggs with the pureed yams. Dip the bread into the mixture and cook on a griddle until both sides are done. (You want to cut down on fried foods for birds.) This is where I also add some calcium, vitamins, spirulina, etc. Try using multi-grain bread instead of whole wheat.

Oatmeal Delight

1/4 fresh banana, mashed
1 tbs. of coconut milk (for thinner
   birds)
1 tsp. finely ground nuts
2-3 strawberries, mashed

1 tsp granola or Grape-Nuts
Yogurt (optional)
1 cup oatmeal
1 3/4 cup water

Mash fruit together. Cook the oatmeal according to instructions. Add the coconut milk to the oatmeal and stir.

Add the mashed fruit. Then add the nuts and stir again. Top with the granola or the Grape-Nuts. Add any flavor of yogurt and stir well. Serve warm.

SUBSTITUTION TIP:
You can substitute a Cream of Wheat package for the oatmeal package.

Eggs and Omelettes

Contents

Carrot Broccoli Omelette

2 eggs with shells (washed)
2 tbs. low-fat ricotta cheese
1/4 cup shredded carrots
1/4 cup finely chopped broccoli

Mix ingredients together. Spray nonstick spray onto frying pan. Scramble eggs until firm.

Birdie Omelette

2 eggs with shells (washed)
2 tbs. low-fat ricotta cheese
1/4 cup shredded carrots
1/4 cup finely chopped broccoli

Mix together. Spray nonstick spray onto frying pan. Scramble eggs until firm.

Eggs Delight

8 large eggs with shells (washed)   1/4 cup chopped spinach
4 tbs. low-fat ricotta cheese   1/4 cup cooked sweet potato
1-2 cups cooked rice or pasta   1/4 cup canned pumpkin
1/4 cup chopped fresh zucchini   2-3 jalapeno peppers, chopped
1/4 cup chopped fresh yellow squash   1 tsp. minced garlic
1/4 cup mixed vegetables

HINT: Try making eggs in the microwave. They come out fluffier and you avoid frying.

Put all ingredients in a microwavable bowl and cook for 8 minutes. You can grate your bird's favorite cheese on top. Sprinkle vitamins on top and cool.

Asparagus, Broccoli, and Cauliflower Omelette

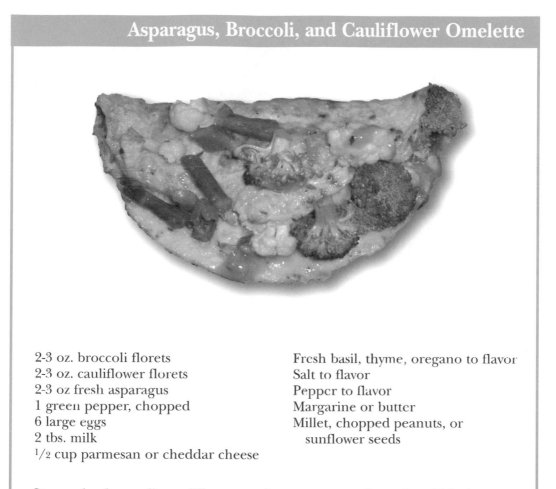

2-3 oz. broccoli florets
2-3 oz. cauliflower florets
2-3 oz fresh asparagus
1 green pepper, chopped
6 large eggs
2 tbs. milk
1/2 cup parmesan or cheddar cheese

Fresh basil, thyme, oregano to flavor
Salt to flavor
Pepper to flavor
Margarine or butter
Millet, chopped peanuts, or
   sunflower seeds

Steam the broccoli, cauliflower, and asparagus until tender. Melt butter or margarine in a pan and add the green pepper. Cook until softened.

Break open the eggs and beat thoroughly, adding the shells if this is only for your birds. (If adding the shells, be sure to wash the eggs first.) Add milk and continue beating. Add seasonings.

Pour mixture into pan (omelette pans work great) and when the mixture starts to thicken, add the steamed vegetables. Add the cheese on top and fold omelette over. Cut into pieces and serve to your bird. If you prefer, you can sprinkle millet, chopped peanuts, or even sunflower seeds over the omelette to garnish.

TIP: Add some crushed red peppers to this for the bird who loves spicy food.

Egg Fu Young

1 can Chinese vegetables
4-6 eggs
1 can baby corn (optional)
Oil

SUBSTITUTION TIPS:
You can add any kind of Chinese vegetable to make Egg Fu Young. I sometimes add bok choy or water chestnuts to this. For the picky eater, add a little millet or sunflower seed to entice him to eat.

Heat oil in frying pan. Mix eggs and vegetables together thoroughly. Pour into hot frying pan. Turn heat down to medium. Cook until lightly brown on one side. Flip over and cook until done on the other side.

This recipe serves several birds as well as several humans. If this is to be used only for your birds, add cleaned eggshells for extra calcium.

A great recipe for people, too!

Pastas and Pizzas

Contents

Polly Pizzas

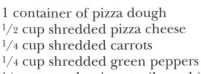

1 container of pizza dough
$^1/_2$ cup shredded pizza cheese
$^1/_4$ cup shredded carrots
$^1/_4$ cup shredded green peppers
$^1/_4$ cup spaghetti sauce (low salt)

Preheat oven to 400°F.

Using a cookie cutter, cut small cookie shapes out of the dough. Cover with sauce, cheese, and veggies. Cook until the cheese is melted (around 5 minutes). Serve warm, not hot!

This recipe is very fast and easy to make, and these are also good snacksfor people.

A great recipe for people, too!

Birdie Pizzas

1 container of pizza dough
$^1/_2$ cup shredded pizza cheese
$^1/_4$ cup shredded carrots
$^1/_4$ cup shredded zucchini
1 jar of baby food

Preheat oven to 350°F.

Using a round cookie cutter, cut out circles on the pizza dough. Spread the jar of baby food on top of shape. Sprinkle with zucchini, carrots, and cheese. Bake for 5-10 minutes or until cheese is bubbly.

WARNING: Never serve anything too hot for your bird. Let it cool down before serving!

When choosing a jar of baby foods, I have found that the spaghetti one works best. You can also use 1-2 tbs. of spaghetti sauce for this.

Millet Mac and Cheese

I was given a female cockatiel that never ate anything but millet before she came to live with me. She was especially stubborn when it came to trying new things. Using this recipe, I got her eating new foods in no time at all. This is a great one for getting small to medium-size birds to try new foods. For larger birds, try chopped sunflowers or pistachio nuts.

1 box any brand macaroni and cheese
$1/2$ cup Kaytee pellets

$1/4$ cup grated carrots
$1/4$ cup chopped broccoli
$1/2$ cup millet

Make the macaroni and cheese according to the instructions on the box. Add in the pellets and the grated carrots. Sprinkle the millet on top, lightly pushing it into the macaroni with the back of a spoon. (My tiels loved the millet and started eating that, but because it was pushed into the macaroni and cheese, they ended up having to eat some of that as well. Now these same tiels will eat anything that I give them.) Putting millet in this dish will entice even the pickiest of birds. (You can also try mega millet for larger birds.)

HELPFUL HINT: If you don't have broccoli, you can add cauliflower or asparagus instead.

Parrot Lasagna

I really like to make this for my birds when I have time, which unfortunately isn't too often. I have found lasagna noodles that you do not have to cook first made by Barilla. This cuts down on the time it takes to make this. Also, there are flavored lasagna noodles you can choose from.

1 box of lasagna noodles	1/4 cup grated carrots
1 jar spaghetti sauce	1 cup yogurt
1 bunch chopped spinach	1/2 cup ricotta cheese
1-2 grated zucchinis	1/4 cup pistachio nuts, chopped
1 cup chopped apples	1/2 cup mozzarella cheese

HINT: If your bird won't eat meat, you can use a little cooked meat in this dish. It hides well.

Preheat oven to 350°F.

Cook noodles according to manufacturer's instructions. In the meantime, combine the ricotta cheese with the yogurt. Add the chopped spinach to this. When the noodles are cooked, spoon some spaghetti sauce on the bottom of a 9x13 pan. Place 2-3 strips of noodles on top of this.

Spread the ricotta/yogurt/spinach mixture for the next layer. Spoon some spaghetti on top of this. Add another layer of noodles. Cover with the chopped apples, adding some spaghetti sauce. Add noodles once again. Then add the grated carrots and spaghetti sauce and another layer of noodles. Sprinkle with pistachio nuts and spaghetti sauce. Then, make a final layer of noodles, finishing with the rest of the spaghetti sauce. Sprinkle the mozzarella cheese.

Bake for 1 hour or until cooked through. Serve when it is cool.

This is a tall, many-layered dish. It is very messy, but birds really love it. Even though you take a long time lovingly preparing this dish, your birds will destroy it in minutes. My beautiful white cockatoo turns red after eating the lasagna. She is a very picky eater but devours this.

Kasha and Bowties

1 cup kasha (buckwheat)
2 cups beef bouillon or broth
1 tsp. margarine

1 package bowtie pasta
1 egg with shell (washed)
Salt

Add the kasha to a beaten egg, coating the kasha lightly. In a large pan, melt the margarine and lightly cook the kasha until it no longer looks wet from the egg. Add the bouillon and stir. Turn heat down to low and continue simmering until all the liquid is absorbed. While that is cooking, make the bowtie pasta according to instructions. When both are done, mix together thoroughly.

This is also a good recipe for people. I always made this for my kids, but Tiny, my macaw, would beg for some. Therefore, I just reduced the amount of salt added, and now it makes a very good bird recipe.

If you are making this recipe for yourself, you can add salt and pepper, and make sure not to include the eggshells. I add a little onion, finely chopped. For your birds you can add peas and carrots instead.

TIP: You can find kasha in the kosher section of your grocery store. Use the coarse grain kasha.

You can also substitute any type of pasta in place of bowtie pasta.

A great recipe for people, too!

Nutty Mac and Cheese

$1/2$ cup pine nuts
1 box any brand macaroni and cheese

Follow instructions on the back of the macaroni and cheese. Add $1/2$ cup of pine nuts and stir. Serve warm.

Easy No-Bake Pizza

1 rice cake low in sugar and salt
1-2 tbs. pizza sauce
Chopped apples
Grated zuchinni

Spread the pizza sauce on top of the rice cake. Add a little chopped apple and grated zucchini. For an added treat, you can substitute chunky peanut butter or any other type of nut butter and top that with your bird's favorite treats. For my Amazon, Charlie, I add peanut butter, sprinkle birdie vitamins that are high in vitamin A, and add grated carrots and chopped pistachio nuts.

This recipe makes a big treat, but my larger birds can handle it fine. Try breaking it up into smaller pieces for smaller birds.

Broccoli Zucchini Pizzas

Whole wheat or regular mini bagels
1-2 tsp. tomato sauce
1 tsp. chopped green peppers
1 tsp. grated zucchini

1 tsp. chopped broccoli
1 clove garlic, crushed
1 tbs. grated parmesan cheese

Preheat oven to 350°F.

Cut mini bagel in half. Spread about 1-2 tsp. tomato sauce on half of the bagel. Add green peppers, zucchini, broccoli, garlic, or whatever vegetable your bird might enjoy. Add cheese and bake until cheese is melted. Serve warm, not hot! You may also add spirulina or vitamins to the finished product.

This recipe is good for 1-2 mini bagels. These are very easy to make and birds love them.

Pasta and Salmon

1 pound mixed-flavors pasta (any type)
1 small can salmon
1/2 cup spaghetti or tomato sauce

Cook pasta according to manufacturer's instructions. Drain. Open can of salmon and drain, removing all bones. Crumble on top of the pasta. Add the tomato or spaghetti sauce. Stir well. Serve warm.

Birdie Pasta

Garden pasta (3 flavors)
Broccoli, chopped
Zucchini, chopped
Celery, chopped
Green peppers, chopped

1 jar of spaghetti sauce
Garlic to taste
1 tbs. parmesan cheese, grated
1 pinch of vitamins (optional)

In a pot with boiling water, add pasta and cook until tender. In microwave, cook vegetables for a few minutes. In another pot, heat spaghetti sauce and add vegetables and garlic. Simmer until vegetables are tender. Drain pasta and add sauce. Sprinkle with cheese and mix thoroughly.

Rice and Noodle Dishes

Contents

Rice Stuffing

Thanksgiving is always a special time at my house. It is an all-day affair, with food coming nonstop. This recipe was adapted from the one I use to serve my guests, but only slightly. For the birds, I use brown rice instead of white rice. My birds really enjoy it.

$^1/_2$ cup wild rice
$^3/_4$ cup brown rice
$^1/_4$ cup white rice
$^1/_2$ cup chopped walnuts
$^1/_4$ cup raisins (golden)
$^1/_4$ cup shredded zucchini

$^1/_4$ cup shredded apple
1 tbs. oil
1 tsp. garlic powder
1 tsp. thyme
1 tsp. parsley

Preheat oven to 350°F.

Cook rice according to instructions. When thoroughly cooked, allow to cool. Saute zucchini in oil until tender, adding water instead of oil if needed. Add to the rice.

Next, add the raisins, apples, nuts, and seasoning. Bake for 15-30 minutes. If it looks like it is drying out, add some water. You can also add bulgur to the rice and cook that; just mix into the rice.

Healthy and tasty, this is also a good recipe for people.

A great recipe for people, too!

Millet, Rice, and Bean Mix

1 cup cooked white rice
1 cup bean mix
1 cup cooked hulled millet
1 cup cooked brown rice

Soak beans overnight. Cook until tender, which takes about 1 hour. Soak millet about 20 minutes while beans are cooking, then add to cooking beans. Drain. Mix together with the rice.

Noodle Kugel (Pudding)

1 bag egg noodles
6 eggs with shells (washed)
1 medium apple, chopped
1/2 cup raisins
Kaytee pellets (optional)
Nuts (optional)
Vitamins/supplements (optional)

Preheat oven to 350°F.

Add noodles to boiling water and cook until done. Drain. Cool slightly. Add eggs with shells, beating well each time. (Only add the shells if you are serving this to your bird only; do not add shells if you will be serving to humans.) Add apple, raisins, pellets, nuts, and supplements. Mix thoroughly.

SUBSTITUTION TIP: Try using golden raisins instead of regular ones. It makes for a different taste.

Pour mixture into a pan that has been coated with spray or vegetable shortening. Bake for 40-60 minutes or until golden brown. Remove, cool, and serve slightly warm.

Noodle kugel is very tasty. After years of making it for my family and having my birds beg for more, I adjusted the recipe for them. If you want to make this for your family, add 1/2 to 1 cup sugar and do not include the shells with the eggs.

A great recipe for people, too!

Pumpkin Seed Risotta

1 cup arberio rice
1-2 zucchini, cut into pieces
2-4 tbs. olive oil

1 cup raw pumpkin seeds
2-4 tbs. parmesan cheese

In a large pan, heat the olive oil. Add the rice and cook until the grains take on a translucent appearance around the edges. Reduce the heat and add 2 cups of the vegetable broth. Stir and cook until most of the broth is reduced.

Add another cup of broth. Keep doing this until rice can no longer absorb the broth. In the microwave, cook the zucchini until done. Add to the rice, mixing often. Add the pumpkin seeds, mixing well. Spoon into your bird's food cup and sprinkle with the cheese.

Beans, Pasta, Rice, and Vegetable Dish

1 cup several different types of grains
1 cup cooked pasta
10 small hot peppers
1 cup brown rice
1 tbs. cinnamon
1 large bag of frozen mixed
    vegetables

$1/2$ cup walnuts, chopped
$1/2$ cup dried cranberries
$1/2$ cup dried mixed fruit, chopped
1 head of garlic, chopped
1 cup 15-bean mix

HINT: You can keep beans in the refrigerator for up to three days.

Cook the grains separately until each one is done. Cook the beans until done. Cook the pasta with five of the hot peppers chopped up and put in the water. Cook the brown rice with the cinnamon.

Boil the chopped onions for around 5-10 minutes and drain. Cook the frozen vegetables. Using enough water to cover, add the dried fruit and cranberries. Drain any extra water. Mix all the ingredients together. Store any extra in baggies in the freezer. Freeze in 2-3 day portions.

When using beans, always make sure they are thoroughly cooked. Never feed beans uncooked. You can also feed sprouted beans.

Sandwiches and Wraps

Contents

Polly Tortillas

1 flour tortilla
2 tbs. peanut butter, chunky or regular
2 tbs. Kaytee pellets
2 tbs. millet
2 tbs. dried red peppers or chili peppers

HELPFUL HINT: Try spinach-flavored or whole-wheat tortillas.

Spread the peanut butter on the tortillas. Cut the tortillas into eight pieces. Mix the pellets, millet, and the peppers together in a bowl. Cover the flour tortilla in this mixture, coating the peanut butter. You can either roll it up or lay the wrap in the bird's bowl.

Palm Nut Tortilla Wraps

1-2 flour tortillas
2 tbs. palm nut pulp
2 tbs. Kaytee pellets

2 tbs. unsalted sunflower seed
2 tbs. mineral block, ground
2 tbs. almonds (opt.)

Hint: I use small budgie or tiel pellets so I don't have to keep grinding up the large pellets.

Spread the palm nut pulp over one side of a flour tortilla. Sprinkle the pellets, sunflower seeds, (optional chopped almonds), and the mineral block powder on top of the palm nut pulp. Roll up tightly. Cut into bird-size pieces.

Calcium Tortilla Wraps

For birds who need extra calcium but turn their beaks up at calcium supplements, this treat will entice even the most finicky of eaters.

1 flour tortilla   Mineral block
Peanut butter, crunchy   Almonds, chopped or sliced

Scrape enough of the mineral block to equal $1/2$ tsp. Set aside. Take enough peanut butter to cover the tortilla. Sprinkle the mineral block powder over the peanut butter. Arrange the sliced or chopped almonds on top. Roll the tortilla tightly. Slice into small pieces, big enough for a snack.

Falafel

1 box falafel mix
1 carrot, finely grated
1 zucchini, finely grated
$1/4$ cup of olive oil

Prepare the falafel according to the manufacturer's instructions. Add the grated carrot and the zucchini and mix well.

In a frying pan, add the oil. When hot, take 1 tbs. of mix and form a patty using two spoons. Carefully drop it into the hot oil. When brown, turn and brown on the other side. Blot on paper towels to soak up any excess oil.

Birdie Sandwiches

1 pita or pocket bread
Sprouts
Cottage cheese or yogurt
Carrots, coarsely grated

Open the pocket bread or the pita bread. Loosely fill with sprouts, carrots, and cottage cheese or yogurt. Cut into eight pieces. Give as a special treat.

Beans and Seeds Mixes

Contents

Soak and Cook

$1/2$ cup soy beans
$1/4$ cup whole green peas
$1/2$ cup paddy rice

$1/4$ cup small beans
$1/4$ cup popcorn (unpopped)

Put all the ingredients in a pan and cover with cold water. Soak for 8 to 12 hours. Drain and cover with hot water, then cook for 1 hour or so. Drain, rinse, and let cool. Cook longer, adding more water when used for small birds. This recipe can be frozen in small, single-size servings for later use.

You can use the 15-bean mix for real variety. The ingredients can be found at a health food store, feed store, or pet food warehouse.

Bean Deluxe

$1/4$ cup pinto beans
$1/4$ cup navy beans
$1/4$ cup kidney beans
$1/4$ cup lentils, cooked
$1/4$ cup yellow or green split peas

1 cup cooked brown rice
1 cup cooked white rice
$1/4$ cup cooked bulgur
1 pkg. frozen veggies
$1/4$ cup banana chips (optional)

Soak the beans overnight. Drain. Add enough water to cover beans and chips. Cook until tender, which usually takes about 1 hour. Add the frozen veggies and continue cooking until done. Drain. Add the previously cooked rice and bulgur.

Beans and Carrots Deluxe

1 pkg. 15-bean soup mix, cooked
1 bag frozen vegetables
1 cup brown rice

1 cup white rice
$1/4$ cup shredded carrot
$1/8$ cup sunflower seeds

TIP: You can freeze small portions of these bean dishes in ice cube trays and just take out what you need.

Soak the beans overnight. Drain. Cook for 1 hour or until tender. Add frozen vegetables and continue cooking for 10-15 minutes more. Add cooked rice. For picky birds, add roasted or raw sunflower seeds (no salt) and mix well.

Pumpkin Seeds

Remove seeds from the pumpkin. Wash them thoroughly, removing any of the fibers of pumpkin. Using a strainer will help because the seeds are slippery. Once washed, pour the seeds onto a dish towel, blotting them dry. (They will stick to paper towels, so if you use them, you will need to pull off the little fabric pieces.)

Next, place the seeds in a bowl and mix them with 1 teaspoon of oil for every cup of seeds. Spread the coated seeds on a cookie sheet and bake for 30-35 minutes. Add salt if you are eating the seeds, but do not add salt for your bird.

Sprouted Seeds

Be sure to purchase untreated seed. Treated seed will not sprout, and seed for planting is treated with an antifungal agent that can make your bird very sick and could even cause death.

For small birds, canary seed, hard red wheat, and/or alfalfa seed work well.

For your larger birds, use sunflower seeds in shells, all types of beans, hard red wheat, alfalfa seed, whole peas, and popcorn seeds.

Place seeds into sprouting jar, rinse well two to three times, draining each time. Fill the jar with lukewarm water. Set the jar in a semi-dark place for 8 hours.

Drain all the water off after this time. Rinse again with lukewarm water at least three times. Drain and turn jar on its side; then shake to make the seeds level in the jar. Be sure the sprout lid has air space. Place the jar in a semi-dark area again for another 8 hours. Also note that seeds will sprout faster in a warm room than a cold room.

Repeat the above step. In another 8 hours, the seeds should be sprouted. If not, rinse with cold water several times and pour in colander to drain. Place in a semi-dark area another 8 hours if this happens. You can feed the sprouts to your birds, rinsing with cold water before serving. Place any extra sprouted seeds in the refrigerator.

Finch Seed Mix

1 part canary seed
1 part hemp
1/2 part white millet
1/2 part Siberian millet

Mix all ingredients together.

You can save money by mixing bird seeds yourself.

Canary Seed Mix

7 parts canary seed
2 parts grape seed
1/2 parts oat groats
1/2 part flax

Mix all ingredients together.

Budgie Seed Mix

2 parts white millet
3 parts canary seed
1 part hemp
1/2 part oat groats
1 part dehydrated vegetables
1 part dehydrated fruit pieces

Mix all ingredients together.

The best seed mixes are the ones you make yourself. Use the Large Hookbill Seed Mix recipe for Macaws.

Mixed Beans, Corn, and Carrot Salad

1 cup cooked mixed beans
1 can corn, drained
2 carrots, thinly sliced

1-2 tbs. olive oil
4-5 tbs. apple cider vinegar
1 tbs. crushed red peppers

Combine the cooked mixed beans, corn, and carrots and mix together. In a small bowl, combine the olive oil, apple cider vinegar, and the crushed red peppers. Mix well. Pour over the beans, corn, and carrot mix and mix well. You can microwave for a minute or until warm, not hot, and serve. Always stir well when you microwave to eliminate hot spots.

Lentils and Pinenut/Almond Salad

$1^1/_2$ cup cooked lentils
3 tbs. apple cider vinegar
1-2 tsp. dijon mustard
1 oz. olive oil

1 oz. walnut oil
$^1/_4$ cup cooked diced chicken
$^3/_4$ cup pinenuts
$^1/_2$ to $^3/_4$ almonds

In a medium bowl, mix together the cooked lentils, apple cider vinegar, mustard, and oil. Stir. Add the pinenuts, almonds, and chicken and mix well. You can microwave for a minute until warm, but not hot. Always stir well when you microwave to eliminate hot spots.

Cockatiel Seed Mix

1 part canary seed
1 part white millet
1 part hemp
2 parts safflower
1 part dehydrated vegetables
1 part dehydrated fruit pieces

For all seed mixes, use fresh seeds. Do not use seeds that are old or webby in appearance.

Mix all ingredients together.

Small Hookbill Seed Mix

1 part canary seed
1 part white millet
3 parts safflower
1 part hemp
1 part oat groats

Mix all ingredients together.

Large Hookbill Seed Mix

1 part pumpkin seeds
1 part canary seed
1 part white millet
3 parts safflower
1 part hemp
1 part oat groats

1 part peanuts
1 part mixed nuts
1 part dehydrated vegetables
1 part dried chili peppers
1 part banana chips

In winter, add one-part sunflower seeds for outdoor birds. This will add extra fat in the diet.

You may also add one-part pine nuts or cracked corn, and $1/2$-part monkey chow may also be added.

Red millet can be substituted for $1/2$ of white millet. This adds more color to the seed. Different types of millet may also be added. You can even add pieces of spray millet, cuttlebone, or pellets.

Parent Bird Seed Mix

1 part peanut hearts
1 part hulled sunflower seeds
1 part hulled pumpkin seeds
1 part millet

For smaller birds, place in a food processor and chop into smaller pieces.

Vegetable Dishes

Contents

Yam Puffs

1 cooked large yam, mashed   Grated apples (for topping)
2 tbs. orange juice   3 tbs. margarine
1 cup Grape-Nuts or granola

Preheat oven to 350°F.

Boil the yams, saving the water you boiled them in. Melt margarine and combine with the mashed yams, orange juice, 1/4 cup of cereal, and, if needed, some of the water from the yams.

Beat well and form into small bite-size balls. Roll in the remaining cereal. Place on a buttered cookie sheet. Top with the grated apples. Bake for about 15 minutes. Cool before serving.

These yam puffs are really tasty. All my birds love them.

Yam Treats

2 large yams, cooked and mashed
1 cup rolled oats
2 grated carrots
1/2 cup carrot juice
1/2 cup golden raisins
1/2 cup chopped peanuts
1 cup whole wheat flour
Water from yams

Preheat oven to 350°F.

Mix ingredients together, adding enough carrot juice or water if batter is too dry. Pour into small muffin pan that is greased. Bake for 20-30 minutes or until a toothpick comes out clean.

Double Baked Potato Treat

1-2 yams
1-2 white potatoes
2 tbs. orange juice

Bake both white potatoes and yams until done. Remove the insides and mash together. Add orange juice to make moist enough to whip. Serve in a little cup when it cools down.

Root Vegetables

$1/2$ lb. yams, diced
$1/2$ lb. red potatoes, diced
$1/2$ lb. carrots, diced
$1/2$ lb. parsnips, diced
$1/2$ lb. beets, diced
3 tbs. olive oil
1-2 cloves garlic, crushed
1-2 tsp. hot chili powder
Pinch of Salt
Pinch of Pepper
2 tbs. chopped cilantro
2-4 tbs. pumpkin seeds
Brown rice

HELPFUL TIP: Always scrub your vegetables thoroughly before using them.

Steam all the vegetables in a large sauce pan. Heat oil in another pan. Add the garlic and spices and cook for 1 minute. Add the vegetables and stir. Cook for 15 minutes.

When tender, add the pumpkin seeds, cooking for 1-2 more minutes. If necessary, add more seasonings. Serve over brown rice.

Root Chips

1 turnip   1 Idaho potato
1 yam   1 large carrot
1 beet   1 celery root
1 red potato   Other root vegetable
1 parsnip   Oil

Potatoes aren't the only root vegetable you can make chips from.

Thoroughly scrub each vegetable. (Make sure there is no green in the potatoes.) Slice each vegetable paper thin. Put paper thin slices in a bowl filled with cold water. When all veggies are sliced, put bowl in the refrigerator for two to three hours.

Heat oil in a deep fryer according to manufacturer's instructions. When the oil reaches the right temperature, add enough vegetable slices to cover the bottom. You do not want to put too much in or they will not cook properly. Fry for a few minutes or until crispy.

Put the fried slices on paper towel to absorb the extra oil. Do not put any salt on these. You can sprinkle some birdie vitamins on them while they are sitting on a paper towel. (Because they are still hot and have some excess oil, vitamins and minerals will stick nicely.)

For a healthier chip, try baking them in the oven. Lightly spray cookie sheet with non-stick spray and bake at 400°F for 15-20 minutes or until chips are crunchy and golden.

Charlie, my Amazon, is a junk-food junkie. He begs for potato chips and other junk food all the time. I made these with him in mind. They are healthier than potato chips, and they are very tasty.

Vegetable Stew

6 cans of low-sodium vegetable broth
1 can kidney beans
1 can navy beans
1 can garbanzo beans (optional)
2 tbs. olive oil
4 cloves garlic
1 large red onion, finely chopped
1 lb. baby carrots
6 stalks celery, finely chopped

1 small green cabbage, chopped
2 cans tomato puree
8 oz. multicolored pasta shapes
1 lb. tofu
5 yams, sliced
6 red potatoes, sliced
1 red pepper, chopped
1 green pepper, chopped
1 yellow pepper, chopped

Lightly sautè garlic, onions, and celery in oil. Add stewed tomatoes and cook on low for 15-20 minutes. Add pasta, broth, peppers, cabbage, yams, and any water that is needed.

Boil for 20-30 minutes. Add beans and tofu. Add water as needed, though you do not want it to be too watery. Spoon into bird's bowls and allow it to cool. Birds do like this still slightly warm. For an extra special treat, sprinkle some grated cheese on top, but not too much.

HELPFUL HINT: If you don't have fresh vegetables available, you can substitute frozen.

Peanut Squash

1 butternut or acorn squash
$1/4$-$1/2$ cup unsalted, shelled peanuts
2-4 tbs. water
Raisins (optional)

Cut the squash into small cubes. Coarsely chop the peanuts. Put into a microwavable dish and stir together. Add the water and cover lightly with waxed paper. Cook until the squash is tender. If you add the raisins, mix thoroughly before cooking. Cool before serving.

Ratatouille

$1/2$ cup olive oil	2 plum tomatoes, diced, skinned,
1 small onion	and seeds removed
1 clove garlic	$1/2$ tsp. rosemary
1 large eggplant	$1/2$ tsp. coliander seeds
2 zucchinis	$1/2$ tsp. basil
1 red pepper	Pinch of pepper
1 green pepper	Pinch of salt
1 yellow pepper	

Slice the zucchini into thin slices. Cut the eggplant into small pieces. Because zucchini and eggplant can sometimes have a bitter taste, put in a shallow dish, sprinkle with salt, and let sit for 30-60 minutes.

Thinly slice the pepper and onion. Crush the garlic. Saute the peppers and onions in the olive oil. When tender, add the eggplant and zucchini. Turn down to low and cover. After 40 minutes, add the tomatoes. (To remove the skin, add to boiling water for around 1-2 minutes. The skin should peel off easily. Cut in half and spoon out the seeds.) Add the rosemary, coliander seeds, basil, salt, and pepper and cook covered for 10-15 more minutes.

Nutty Salsa

1 large eggplant, chopped
2 large zucchinis, chopped
4 stalks celery, chopped
6 large tomatoes, chopped
3-4 large cloves of garlic, chopped
1 tsp. fresh basil
1 tsp. fresh oregeno
$1/4$ tsp. fresh thyme

1 green pepper, chopped
2 large hot peppers, chopped
1 cup pine nuts
1 cup shelled pistachio
1 tsp. salt
$1/2$ cup olive oil
$1/4$ cup sugar
$1/3$ cup apple cider vinegar

In a large pot, heat the olive oil; then add the chopped eggplant, celery, green peppers, and hot peppers. Saute until tender. Add the pine nuts and pistachios. Cook for 3-5 minutes more on a low heat. Remove and set aside.

In another pan, add the chopped tomatoes, garlic, salt, basil, oregano, and thyme. Cook for 5-10 minutes on medium heat. Fold into the pine-nut mixture. Using the same sauce pan, heat the vinegar and sugar on low, dissolving the sugar. Add the pine-nut/tomato mixture, stirring to coat.

I usually serve this mixed with a pasta or with brown rice.

Carrot Apple Special

2 cups chopped or shredded carrots
5 apples, sliced (peeled and cored)
2 tbs. flour, preferrably whole wheat

4 tbs. honey
4 tbs. margarine
$3/4$ cup orange or apple juice

Preheat oven to 350°F.

Place sliced apples in a baking dish and cover with the carrots. Sprinkle flour over the top. Drizzle honey on top of the flour. Pour juice over the entire dish and bake for 45 minutes.

Baked Pumpkin

1 4-lb pumpkin

Cut a 3-inch circle around the stem and remove. Then remove the seeds. (Use the seeds for pumpkin seed recipes.) Placing the pumpkin on a cookie sheet, bake for 1-1½ hours or until it is tender. Pierce with a fork to check if it is done.

TIP: At Halloween, buy an extra pumpkin for your bird. While the kids are busy carving theirs, you can cook one for your bird. Save the seeds for an extra treat. (See the recipe for Pumpkin Seeds.)

You can also cut the pumpkin in quarters and place face down on a buttered cookie sheet. Cool. Use the leftover pumpkin in recipes or serve as is. You can freeze the leftovers.

This is an excellent food for weaning baby birds and for parent birds feeding babies. I have a friend who serves this on top of Zwieback teething cookies. She will sometimes soak the Zwieback and then add it into the mix.

For older birds who are hard to get interested in new foods, I have found that sprinkling millet or chopped nuts on top will encourage them to eat.

Baked Potato Treat

1-2 potatoes, washed and scrubbed
Chopped broccoli
1-2 tsp. cheddar cheese
Small amount of yogurt

Bake potatoes until done. Chop up broccoli and shred cheese. Scoop out the inside of potatoes and mash it well. Mash in cheese and broccoli. Add yogurt to make it more moist. Put this mixture back into skin. Give small amount to each bird.

Taboule and Vegetables

1 bag of mixed vegetables
$^1/_2$-1 cup of cooked squash, cut into small pieces
$^3/_4$ cup chopped nuts
1 box of Taboule (I use the Near East brand)

Mix the taboule according to the manufacturer's instructions. Just before serving, add the vegetables, squash, and nuts, and mix together well. Serve warm.

Mash Diets

Contents

Mash Diet

1 bag of frozen vegetables (mixed)
1 yam (cooked)
1 potato
$^1/_4$ cup split yellow peas
$^1/_4$ cup split green peas
$^1/_4$ cup pinto beans
$^1/_4$ cup kidney beans
$^1/_4$ cup garbanzo beans
$^1/_4$ cup brown rice,
$^1/_4$ cup wheat berries
$^1/_4$ cup pearl barley
$^1/_4$ cup triticale

1 large leaf of mustard greens
1 small banana
$^1/_2$ apple
10 grapes
5 strawberries
$^1/_8$ cup cranberries (fresh if available)
$^1/_8$ cup mixed pumpkin seeds
$^1/_8$ cup sesame seeds
Optional: hard boiled egg with shell, peanuts, seedling grass, almonds, and/or orange pieces.

This is a great weaning diet that I created using recipes from several different breeders. While there were several differences between all the different recipes, I combined many of the ingredients that I knew my birds liked and came up with this one.

Cook beans and rice until almost done, add potato and yam slices, and cook until potatoes are tender. Then, add mixed vegetables. In a food processor, add mustard greens, apple, strawberries, and cranberries. Process for a few seconds. Add warm cooked mix. Process for a few more seconds, until a mash is acquired. Mash in banana by hand. Serve warm.

Bean and Veggie Mash

16 oz. 15-bean soup mix
2 ripe bananas
4 yams
4 tbs. margarine

1 small can of pumpkin (1/2 of large can)
1 cup frozen vegetables
Baby carrots
Water, as needed

Soak the 15-bean mix for at least 3 hours in cold water. Rinse thoroughly and put them in a large saucepan, cover with water, and cook for 20 minutes. Add the bananas (cut into small pieces), yams, and frozen vegetables.

Cook until all the vegetables are tender. Drain off excess water. In a separate bowl, mash the vegetables together and add the canned pumpkin. Sprinkle with vitamins, minerals, spirulina, etc. Serve warm.

FACT: Mash diets are great for weaning babies. They are also excellent for parent birds.

Mish Mash

2 cups cooked brown rice
1 can pumpkin
2 cups frozen vegetables
1 cup any kind cooked beans

1 large red apple
1 large Granny Smith apple
Some fresh spinach

Cook the rice and the beans until done. Place in a food processor and finely chop. Add the apples and vegetables and continue to chop up finely. Remove from the processor. Wash the spinach and place in food processor and chop.

Open the can of pumpkin and mix with all the other ingredients. Put in ice cube trays and freeze. Remove individual cubes and thaw. Warm in the microwave. Serve with a sprinkle of vitamins, minerals, spirulina, etc.

Fruit Dishes, Desserts, and Treats

Contents

Parrot Candy

$^1/_2$ lb. dates
$^1/_2$ lb. dried apricots
$^1/_2$ lb. dried figs
$^1/_2$ lb. mixed dried fruit

2 cups chopped walnuts
$^1/_2$ cup cranberry and raisin mix
1 tsp: sesame seeds or hulled
   buckwheat

Put dates, figs, walnuts, apricots, mixed dried fruit, raisins, and cranberries through a food grinder. Grind. Scoop out and shape into small balls. Roll in seeds, buckwheat, or finely chopped nuts. Refrigerate portions until ready to feed.

Optional: Try mixed nuts or pistachio nuts in place of walnuts.

This recipe is very tasty, but messy to make. I keep a batch in the refrigerator and take out what I need, rolling it in either sesame seeds or chopped nuts.

Parrot Popsicles

This is one of Tiny's favorite recipes. He loves to crunch ice cubes, especially on hot days, and he loves the fresh fruit and juice in the popsicles. Kids may even enjoy this recipe.

1 small banana
$^1/_4$ cup watermelon
1 large apple, cored
$^1/_4$ cup honeydew melon
$^1/_4$ cup cantaloupe

$^1/_4$ cup crenshaw melon
1 cup strawberries
30 grapes (red, green or mixed)
1 orange

Thoroughly wash all ingredients. Place the fruit into a juicer. Save the pulp. Mix with the juice, adding water if necessary. Pour into ice cube trays. You can add vitamins to this if you do not plan on feeding this recipe to humans.

A great recipe for people, too!

Fruit Salad

You can mix any and all of the following ingredients together for a fruit salad. Note that some of these are seasonal fruits and may be difficult to find during certain times of the year.

Medium apples, peeled and core removed
1 small banana, peeled
1 pear, peeled and core removed
5-10 strawberries
2 kiwis, peeled
1 orange, peeled and any seeds removed
1/4 cantaloupe seeds, rind removed
1/4 honeydew, rind removed
1/4 cup blueberries
1/4 cup raspberries
10 green grapes
10 red grapes
10 black grapes
1/2 mango, skinned
1/4 cup raisins
1/2 papaya, skinned
1/2 cup walnuts, coarsely chopped
1/2 cup cranberries

Remove the skin, pits, or seeds from any fruit. Cut into small pieces or chop finely for smaller birds. Mix together well and store in an air tight container and place in the refrigerator.

If berries are in season, you can add blackberries or raspberries in addition to the strawberries and blueberries. I buy fresh cranberries and freeze them so I always have some on hand. You can pour some unsweetened fruit juice over the fruit before serving. This helps especially in hot weather to give them the extra liquids that they need. When I do this, I remove their cups after one hour. Things spoil faster in the summer than they do in the winter.

FACT: If your bird is eating a lot of fruit, he may not be drinking as much water. He is getting his water from the fruit.

A great recipe for people, too!

Gooey Banana Treats

> 1 banana, peeled
> 2 tbs. crunchy peanut butter
> $^{1}/_{2}$ cup unsalted chopped pistachios

In the microwave, melt the peanut butter for around 1 minute. Cut the banana into quarters. Roll the banana in the melted peanut butter. Roll the peanut-butter covered bananas in the chopped pistachios.

This is a very messy treat. I use wooden candy sticks, which gives the birds something to hold onto.

Birdie Kabobs

1 bird kabob toy
Grapes
Apple slices
Banana slices
Strawberries

Kiwi slices
Melon slices
Lemon juice, enough to brush on
    the fruit to keep it from turning
    brown.

Alternate fruit on the kakob and hang in the bird's cage. Remove after two hours.

Travel Kabobs

These kabobs are great for traveling with your bird.

Kabob sticks
1 banana, sliced
10 grapes

10 strawberries
1 apple, cut into wedges
Lemon juice

Thread fruit onto the kabob sticks in any order. Brush with the lemon juice. Store in a cooler when traveling with your bird.

Banana Treats

1 ripe banana	Millet (mega millet for larger birds)
Vitamin and mineral supplements	Sunflower seeds
Spirulina	Chopped nuts

Mix together the proper amount of supplements for your bird. Lightly roll the sliced banana in the mix. Next, roll in the millet, sunflower seeds, or chopped nuts. Make sure that you push down slightly so it really sticks to the banana and that they have to eat some of the banana to get to the treat. This will depend on what your bird enjoys most. For my smaller birds, I use millet. My medium-sized birds enjoy a combination of mega millet and sunflower seeds, and my larger birds enjoy the sunflower seed/chopped nut mixture.

Cheesy Fruit Salad

1 tsp. salt	3 kiwi
$1/2$ cup shredded cheddar cheese	1 banana
1 small pineapple	$1/2$ cup apple juice
1 tangerine	$1/2$ cup orange juice
1 mango	$1/2$ cup guava nectar
1 papaya	Unflavored yogurt
2 star fruits	Fresh mint

Peel and core pineapple. Then peel and remove seeds from the tangerine. Peel and pit the mango. Peel and remove seeds from the papaya.

Add cheese, place in a food processor, and chop into medium chunks. Drain, removing juice. Save the juice. Slice the kiwis, star fruits, and the banana. Mix all the juices together. Pour over the fruits. Add yogurt and stir. Garnish with fresh mint. (You can use peppermint, spearmint, or other mint flavors.)

Sprinkle the cheddar cheese on top.

Because lories and lorikeets are nectar eaters, this recipe and other fruit dishes would probably be particularly beneficial to them.

Apple Delight

4 apples, peeled and quartered
2 tbs. wheat germ
$^1/_4$ cup raisins
$^1/_4$ cup Grape-Nuts

$^1/_4$ cup granola
$^1/_4$ tsp. cinnamon
$^1/_4$ cup chopped walnuts
1-2 cups apple juice

Preheat oven to 350°F.

Peel and core the apples. Cut the apples into quarters. Combine the wheat germ, Grape Nuts, raisins, granola, cinnamon, and walnuts with the apples. Mix well. Place this into a baking dish that has been sprayed with a non-stick coating. Pour juice over the apple mixture. Bake for around 45 minutes.

This is also a tasty treat for people.

A great recipe for people, too!

Summer Fruit Salad

This recipe is perfect for a hot summer's day.

1 medium orange, peeled and
    segmented
1 medium tangerine, peeled and
    segmented
1 banana, peeled and sliced
20 red grapes

20 green grapes
1 cup fresh strawberries, cut in half
$^1/_2$ cup blueberries and/or
    raspberries
1 small apple, peeled and sliced
1 mango, peeled and sliced

FACT: If your bird eats a lot of fruit, such as strawberries, his droppings may appear red. Do not panic. Once the fruit is out of his system, his droppings will return to normal.

Combine all ingredients and toss well. This can also be put into a juicer and then put into ice cube trays and frozen. Makes a great treat especially for birds who love to eat ice. Other birds love eating the treat in a cup.

Birdie Treats

          Pumpkin seeds
          Barley
          Oats
          Sesame seeds
          Millet
          Tomatoes
          Apples
          Bananas
          Grapes
          Lemons
          Oranges
          Carrots (lightly steamed)
          Corn
          Spinach

Put the bananas, apples, lemons, and oranges (minus rinds and peel) into a food processor. Chop. In a separate bowl, put the seeds, barley, and oats; mix. Add the chopped fruit. Add grapes.

In the food processor, add carrots and corn and finely chop. Add the spinach and continue chopping. Mix all together and serve. Put remaining treats in an icecube tray and freeze.

Parent Bird Treats

        Zweiback toast
        Apple juice or water
        1 pinch of spirulina
        1 pinch of vitamin/mineral supplement

Pour juice or water over the toast. Microwave until warm. Sprinkle spirulina and vitamin/mineral supplement over the warmed toast. Mash up. Cool until warm (not hot). Feed to parent birds.

Birdie Soft Treats

1 cup dried whole corn
1 cup mixed beans, cooked
1 cup brown rice
1/2 cup mixed nuts, chopped
1/2 cup whole oats
1/2 cup flavored macaroni

2 medium yams, cooked and mashed
1/2 cup dried mixed fruit, chopped
1/2 can of pumpkin
Shelled pumpkin seeds, chopped
   (optional)

Overnight, soak whole corn. Drain, rinse, and add more water. Cook for several hours, adding more water as needed. It is done when it is soft in the center. Also overnight, soak mixed beans. Drain, rinse, and add more water. Cook until tender.

Cook brown rice according to manufacturer's instructions. Add nuts, fruit, and pumpkin seeds to the cooking macaroni. Cook oats according to manufacturer's instructions. Add all ingredients together, mixing well, and allow to cool. Freeze leftovers in individual serving-size baggies. This is high in vitamin A and is good for all birds.

HELPFUL HINT:
Always rinse beans several times after soaking them overnight.

Pistachio Treats

1 cup dried mixed fruit
1/2 cup uncooked oatmeal
1/2 cup fresh cranberries
1/2 cup chopped pistachio nuts,
   unsalted

1 tbs. almond butter
1 tbs. bee pollen
1 tbs. honey

Preheat oven to 350°F.

In a food processor, chop the first four ingredients. Add the bee pollen next and process until well mixed. This is a very sticky batter. Add the remaining ingredients and stir by hand until it gets too thick.

On a lightly floured board, knead the mix until it becomes easily rollable. Make 1/2 inch balls and place them on a cookie sheet. Bake for 20 minutes or until done. Cool and serve.

Parrot Pudding

1 cup finely ground corn flour
1-2 cups water
$^1/_2$ cup canned pumpkin

$^1/_2$ cup apple sauce
Vitamins or supplements

Boil water and add corn flour. Stir. If too thick, add more water until it is more liquid than solid. (This is similar to making pudding. When you first add the liquid, it is very thin and wet, but when you cook it, it thickens.) Stir until it thickens like a pudding, making sure it is not too dry.

Add pumpkin and applesauce and cook for around two to three more minutes. Add vitamins, minerals, and/or supplements. Pour leftovers into an ice cube tray and freeze. Once frozen, pop treats into a baggie and put back into the freezer.

This recipe is great for all birds. You may even want to teach your bird to eat this off a spoon that you are holding. If you need to medicate your bird, this is a good place to hide the medicine.

HELPFUL HINTS: Parent birds need healthy, nutritious meals more than ever. You can give this Parrot Pudding recipe to them several times a day. If you do, cut back on the spirulina and vitamins.

Sneak Treats

Apple, peeled, cored, and cut in quarters
Peanut butter
Millet

Take peanut butter and spread it thinly onto the apple. Roll in the millet.

This is a good way to introduce birds to new foods. Foods that allow the millet to stick easily won't need peanut butter. As the bird eats the millet, he is also tasting the peanut butter and the apple (or other food).

Pumpkin Birdie Pie

Pastry
1 cup wheat flour
$1/4$ cup oil
2 tbs. water
1 egg

Filling
Small can of pumpkin
$1/4$ cup honey
$1/2$ tsp. cinnamon (fresh ground is best)
$1/2$ tsp. ginger
$1/2$ tsp. cloves
3 eggs
1 cup milk
6 oz. unsweetened evaporated milk

HELPFUL HINT: You can use a pre-made pie crust to save time. If you have some time on your hands, use fresh pumpkin instead. If you want to make this for yourself as well, increase the honey to $3/4$ cup. Remember, birds do not need extra sugar.

Preheat oven to 400°F.

To make the pie shell, mix all ingredients under pastry together and roll out into dough. Line a greased pie pan with the dough. Mix the remaining ingredients together and pour into the shell. Bake for 50 minutes. Cook until a toothpick inserted comes out clean.

A great recipe for people, too!

Special Treats

2 cups yellow corn meal
1 cup multi grain flour
$1/2$ cup raisins
$1/2$ cup cranberries
1 cup mixed nuts, unsalted
$3/4$ cup raw sunflower seeds

$1/4$ cup peanuts (unsalted)
1 large can solid packed pumpkin
32 oz.-bottle of papaya nectar
$1/2$ cup walnut oil
1 tsp. ground cinnamon
1 tbs. baking powder

Preheat oven to 425°F.

Combine ingredients in a large bowl, adding water to make a pourable batter. Pour into 2 greased and floured baking pans. Bake for around 25-30 minutes or until done. This is a heavy bread and it can be frozen. All birds love it, but Eclectus seem to really enjoy this bread.

Snacks

Contents

Almond Butter

1 pound almonds (roasted)
$1/4$-$1/2$ tsp. oil

The oil is only needed to make a smoother, moister nut butter. In a food processor with steel-blades, blend almonds until you get a smooth, buttery texture. Scrape down sides frequently. You can substitute cashews, hazelnuts, pistachios, etc. for the almonds.

This makes a tasty treat for you or your bird. You may want to add a little salt and use this as a recipe for yourself. It makes a great change from peanut butter.

A great recipe for people, too!

Birdie Party Mix

Chex, wheat, rice, corn, or mixed
Cheerios, any type
Kix, regular or berry
Shredded wheat, regular, or fruit-
   filled
Corn puffs
Grape-Nuts
Peanuts (not in shell, unsalted)
Pretzels (salt-free)

Raisins
Mixed, dried fruit
Goldfish crackers (low salt)
Popcorn, natural, popped
Chopped mixed nuts (no salt)
Spray millet, broken into small
   pieces
Pine nuts, no shells
Banana chips
1 Kaytee treatster bar, broken into
   small pieces

HELPFUL HINT: You can turn many of your favorite recipes into birdie recipes by adjusting, eliminating, or adding different ingredients. Just remember—birds do not need the added sugars or salts.

These can all be mixed together in whatever portions you want. Go lightly on the cereals that are higher in sugar. This keeps nicely in an airtight container. You can also add anything else that your bird enjoys. This can be served daily in a little treat cup or on special occasions.

Healthy Popcorn

1 bag of natural popcorn
Nonstick spray
Minerals

Vitamins (optional)
Spirulina
Wheat grass

Spray the popped popcorn with the nonstick spray. Mix minerals, vitamins, spirulina, and wheat grass thoroughly, according to the amounts needed. Place in a salt shaker. Shake over the popcorn that is sprayed.

You can also get a new vitamin spray that contains spirulina. This spray would be substituted for the vitamins, spirulina, and the nonstick spray.

Birdie Trail Mix

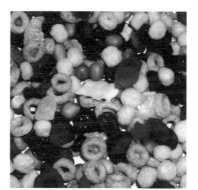

1 part dried berries
1 part dried mixed fruit
1 part raisins
1 part Cheerios

1 part Kix
1 part unsalted
peanuts

For a quick and healthy snack, try Kaytee Treatsters. Treatsters are healthy, granola bar treats for birds and come in Forest Nut, Papaya Nut, and Tropical Fruit flavors.

Mix all ingredients together and store in an air-tight plastic container.

This is a quick-and-easy snack to make for short road trips. I take my birds with me sometimes and I like to bring a little snack along for them.

Wheat Grass

Start with either winter wheat berries or hard wheat berries. Both can be found in a health food store.

Rinse the wheat berries and place them in a bowl or a wide-mouth jar. Cover them with water. Cover the bowl with a towel or, preferably, cheesecloth, and let sit at least 12 hours.

Rinse the wheat berries. Let them remain wet but not soaking in water for another 12 hours. Rinse at least once more during the 12-hour period. You should start seeing the berries beginning to sprout. You will now need to plant them. Go to the nursery and buy some flats and plant them in 1 inch of soil. Don't overwater.

From start to finish, this will take around one week.

Pine Cones

Pine cones make great snack-toys for your bird. They will keep them entertained for hours.

Make sure the pine cones are not old, damp, moldy, mossy, or have anything else on them. Make sure that no little creatures such as spiders or other insects have made a home inside. You can kill off molds and little inhabitants by heating them in the oven for around 20 minutes at 225°F, but this will not sterilize them. Do not exceed 225°F because the pine cones may then catch on fire.

You can take some peanut butter and smear it on the pine cones and then roll the cones in seeds, such as millet, crunched peanuts, or mixed nuts or sunflower seeds.

Meats

Contents

Chicken Soup

This soup is delicious for both humans and birds alike. It is an old family recipe.

> 2 4-lb. chickens cut up into 6-8 pieces
> 4 whole onions, quartered
> 2 lbs. of carrots or baby carrots
> 2 heaping tbs. crushed or minced garlic
> 2 whole stalks celery, cut into pieces
> 3 chicken bouillon cubes
> Pepper to taste
> Salt, pinch for birds
> 2 tbs. salt for humans (optional)
> 1 pinch of onion powder (optional)
> Dehydrated vegetables (optional)
> Enough water to cover (Usually 20-24 cups of water)

Cook the chickens, onions, carrots, and celery in the water. Bring to a boil; then turn down to a medium-low fire. Cook 3-4 hours or until the chicken falls apart when you lift it and the water level drops around 2-3 inches.

Remove any of the foaming material that forms on top. When done cooking, allow to cool slightly. Drain the liquid broth off into a large pot. Add the cooked carrots to the broth. The celery, onions, carrots, and chunks of chicken can be mashed up for your birds.

Remove the skin when you cut up the chicken. Save the leg bones, thigh bones, and the bones from the wings. To the broth, add the bouillon cubes, pepper, and garlic. Set some of this aside for your birds. For your remaining broth, add salt to taste. You can also add onion powder and dehydrated vegetables to the broth that you set aside for your birds.

A great recipe for people, too!

Chicken Soup Additions

Noodles

Add one bag or box of noodles to boiling water and cook on medium heat until tender. Drain and rinse with cold water. Add to soup.

Rice

Add 1 cup of rice to 2 cups of boiling water. Turn heat down to low and cover. Cook until all of the water is absorbed. You may not want to add this directly to the soup because the rice will continue expanding.

Matzoh Balls

In a bowl, beat four eggs. Add 2 tbs. oil and 2 tbs. broth from the chicken soup. Beat well. Beat in 2 cups of matzoh meal, beating well each time. Add salt and pepper to taste. Place bowl in the refrigerator for two hours.

Right before you remove this mixture, have a pot of water on the stove. Start to boil the water. Remove from the refrigerator–the mixture will have thickened some while cooling.

Wetting your hands, place an egg-sized amount of the matzoh meal mixture in your hands and roll into a ball shape. Put this into the boiling water. Repeat until you have no more mixture left. Turn water down to a medium to medium-low heat. Cook around 30 minutes. With a slotted spoon, remove each matzoh ball, one at a time, and place in the chicken broth.

This was Rocky's favorite weaning food, but because he kept climbing on top of them and eating them from the bottom, they kept rolling on him. We ended up making Matzoh squares for him instead.

Egg Drops

Egg drops are simply eggs, salt, and flour mixed together until a loose dough is formed. The dough is sticky, but it will not run off a spoon.

Scoop one heaping tablespoon of the dough and drop it into boiling water. (You will find it easier to put the spoon into the boiling water and allowing the dough to fall off this way.) These are like dumplings. Turn the heat down to medium to medium-low and cook for 15-20 minutes.

Kreplach

Kreplach is for the more ambitious cook. It is great for leftover roast, particularly brisket. Grind up any leftover cooked brisket, putting it through the grinder twice. Sautè onions in olive oil, and once the onions are golden brown, run them through the grinder twice as well. Mix thoroughly. You may have to add more salt and pepper.

Beat several eggs, salt, and pepper until well blended. Add enough flour to make a dough stiff enough to roll out. Roll dough out in thin layers. With a sharp knife, cut out square-shaped pieces large enough to hold 1 tbs. full of meat mixture. Add meat. Fold square in half and pinch closed, so the meat won't fall out. Make sure you have a good seal. You now have a little meat pocket. Repeat until all the meat is gone. (Don't roll the dough so thinly that the meat breaks the dough).

In a large pot, boil water. Gently add kreplach to the boiling water. Reduce heat to medium. Boil 20-30 minutes. Carefully drain. You can also use a slotted spoon to remove. Add to the soup.

Kreplach is very versatile and can be stretched very far. You can also make this with chicken instead of beef.

You can also add margarine or oil to an oven-safe pan and bake for 30 minutes at 375°F until golden. Some people also deep fry kreplach in oil.

Chicken Bones

The chicken bones you set aside while making the soup are great for your birds. I give the large leg and thigh bones to my larger birds, which they crack open. The smaller birds get the wing bones.

Vegetables

For my smaller birds, I chop vegetables up into a fine mash, then add some of the broth. I then add either the noodles, rice, egg drops, matzoh balls or kreplach to this, also mashing it well. Frozen veggies can be thawed, mashed, and added also.

Stir-Fry Beef/Chicken With Peanuts

3 oz. chicken or beef
8 oz. broccoli florets
1 can baby corn, drained
1 can bean sprouts, drained
4 oz. fresh sugar snap peas
1 green pepper, thinly sliced
1 clove garlic, crushed

1-2 cups bok choy, chopped (spinach is okay)
1-2 tbs. wok oil (vegetable oil is okay)
1/4 cup peanuts
1 bunch green onions
1 tablespoon soy sauce
Dried peppers

WARNING: Always thoroughly cook any kind of meat, poultry, or fish before giving any to your bird.

Thinly slice the beef or the chicken. Add oil to the wok and, once hot, add the beef or chicken. Cook until all pink is out of the meat. Remove meat with slotted spoon. Drain. Add more oil. Add broccoli, sugar snap peas, green pepper, green onions, and bok choy. Stir-fry until crisp.

Add bean sprouts, baby corn, garlic, and peanuts. Add dried peppers and stir. Add beef or chicken and stir-fry for 3-5 minutes. Add soy sauce and stir-fry for 1-2 more minutes. Serve with brown rice, white rice, stir-fried rice, or even noodles.

Stir-fry is a fast and easy way to cook for your bird. You can make this with or without the meat. This is an excellent recipe for both you and your birds to share. My birds like it when I use Thai pepper sauce when I make this. I serve it over stir-fried or steamed rice or noodles. You can increase the amount of meat for yourself if sharing with your birds.

A great recipe for people, too!

Carrot Chicken Balls

4 lbs. yams, boiled and mashed
2 hard-boiled eggs
1 tbs. vegetable oil
1/4 cup boiled mashed carrots
Carrot juice

1 skinless chicken breast, boiled
3 cups high-fiber, low-fat bread crumbs
1 tbs. palm nut pulp or palm oil
1 tsp. bee pollen

Finely chop up the chicken breast. Mix all the ingredients together with enough water to hold the mix together. Form into balls.

This is a great recipe for the leftover chicken breast and carrots from the soup.

Nutty Salmon Corn Muffins

1 can of cornmeal muffin mix or 2 boxes
of corn muffin mix
1 cup of sliced or chopped almonds
1 package of salmon (A package of
salmon dried and specially prepared for
birds can be ordered from Smiles of
Feathers at www.smilesoffeathers.com.)
$1/4$-$1/2$ cup pine nuts

Mix the muffin mix according to the manufacturer's instructions. Stir in the almonds and continue mixing. Add the salmon to the muffin and stir well.

Preheat the oven to 400°F. Spray muffin pan with nonstick spray. Bake for 30 minutes or until a toothpick comes out clean.

Not only is salmon an excellent source of omega-3, but it is also contains all the essential amino acids. In addition, salmon contains vitamins A, D, B6, and B2, as well as niacin, riboflavin calcium, iron, zinc, magnesium, and phosphorus.

Resources

ORGANIZATIONS

American Federation of Aviculture

P.O. Box 7312

N. Kansas City, MO 64116

Telephone: (816) 421-2473

Fax: (816) 421-3214

E-mail: afaoffice@aol.com

http://www.afa.birds.org/

Avicultural Society of America

P.O. Box 5516

Riverside, CA 92517-5516

Telephone: (909) 780-4102

Fax: (909) 789-9366

E-mail: info@asabirds.org

http://www.asabirds.org/index.php

Aviculture Society of the United Kingdom

Arcadia-The Mounts-East Allington-Totnes

Devon TQ9 7QJ

United Kingdom

E-mail: admin@avisoc.co.uk

http://www.avisoc.co.uk/

British Bird Council

1st Floor Offices

1159 Bristol Road South

Northfield, Birmingham, B31 2SL

Telephone: 44 01214-765999

http://www.britishbirdcouncil.com/

Smiles of Feathers

3401 Prill Road

Centralia, WA 98351

Telephone: (360) 736-3973

E-mail: smiles@localaccess.com

http://www.smilesoffeathers.com/index.tpl

PUBLICATIONS

Bird Talk Magazine

3 Burroughs

Irvine, CA 92618

Telephone: (949) 855-8822

Fax: (949) 855-3045

http://www.animalnetwork.com/birdtalk/default.asp

Bird Times Magazine

7-L Dundas Circle

Greensboro, NC 27407

Telephone: (336) 292-4047

Fax: (336) 292-4272

E-mail: info@petpublishing.com

http://www.petpublishing .com/birdtimes/

Pet & Aviary Birds Magazine

P.O. Box 30806

Knoxville, TN 37930-0806

Telephone: (800) 487-3333

Fax: (865) 690-4941

http://www.petandaviarybirds.com/

Winged Wisdom Magazine

Birds n Ways

39760 Calle Bellagio

Temecula, CA 92592

Telephone: (909) 303-9376

http://www.birdsnways.com/wisdom/index.htm#toc

INTERNET RESOURCES

Exotic Pet Vet. Net

(http://www.exoticpetvet.net)

This website, authored by an avian veterinarian and an aviculturist/zoologist, offers extensive information on a variety of bird-related topics, including nutrition, health, and emergency care.

HolisticBird.org

(http://www.holisticbird.org)

HolisicBird.org maintains that the mental, emotional, and spiritual wellness of a bird's whole being is directly tied to health. With this belief in mind, HolisticBird.org provides information on diet, nutrition, healing, and behavior from a holistic perspective.

VETERINARY RESOURCES

Association of Avian Veterinarians (AAV)

P.O. Box 811720

Boca Raton, FL 33481-1720

Telephone: (561) 393-8901

Fax: (561) 393-8902

E-mail: AAVCTRLOFC@aol.com

http://www.aav.org/

EMERGENCY RESOURCES AND RESCUE ORGANIZATIONS

ASPCA Animal Poison Control Center

Telephone: (888) 426-4435

E-mail: napcc@aspca.org (for non-emergency, general information only)

http://www.apcc.aspca.org

Bird Hotline

P.O. Box 1411

Sedona, AZ 86339-1411

E-mail: birdhotline@birdhotline.com

http://www.birdhotline.com/

Feathered Friends Adoption and Rescue

222 S.W. Dillon Ct.

Port St. Lucie, FL 34953-6203

Telephone: (772) 343-8935

Fax: (772) 344-7237

E-mail: jesbirds@msn.com

http://hometown.aol.com/MAHorton/FFAP.html

Index